B.C.

by Dale S. Crowley

1502 ANSWERS TO BIBLE QUESTIONS

SUNRISE IN THE NATION'S CAPITAL

RED WORLD REVOLUTION

THE CURSE OF A NATION

GEMS I LOVE TO SHARE

The Soon Coming
of
Our Lord

"Even so, Come, Lord Jesus," Rev. 22:20

By DALE CROWLEY, D. D.,

Washington's Radio Minister

NEW YORK
LOIZEAUX BROTHERS

DEDICATION

To my two preacher sons—DALE PATRICK and ROBERT DANIEL, with the fervent prayer that during the closing days of this age they may reap a harvest of souls as they continue to faithfully declare the whole counsel of God, anticipating that day when "we shall all appear before the judgment seat of Christ," this volume is affectionately dedicated.

PREFACE

In a Sunday afternoon series of radio messages to a Washington, D. C. area audience, under the general theme, "Bible Prophecy and the End of the Age," a gratifying interest in the subject has been stimulated. The chapters in this book represent the substance of as many talks given over the air, with minor additions, and are sent forth in this form because of the request of many listeners.

It is our sincere conviction that the study of prophecy, and more particularly those prophecies dealing with our Lord's return, will have a transforming effect in the lives of God's people. With the over-all perspective of God's great plan, we are made aware that our constant objective is to rightly relate ourselves to God's program, and seek through the aid of the blessed Holy Spirit to fulfill His will.

Thus, in the anticipation of our Lord's return, we do not make the mistake of becoming curious "star gazers" but, rather, living witnesses for our Lord, here and now. If our Lord delays His coming for one year, or for one day, it is in order to give to us who love His appearing an opportunity to further serve Him by witnessing to a needy world.

The night is far spent; the day is at hand. "The coming of our Lord draweth nigh."

—DALE CROWLEY.

P. O. Box One,
Washington, D. C.

CONTENTS

I   The Priceless Value of a Precious Truth

The Priceless Value of a Precious Truth

"Looking for that blessed hope, and the glorious appearing of the great God and our Saviour Jesus Christ," Titus 2:13.

One who studies the Scriptures is impressed with the tremendous importance of the doctrine of our Lord's return in relation to the entire body of revealed truth. The prominent place which this teaching occupies in the Word of God produces in our hearts the feeling that our Heavenly Father certainly intended it to be so.

Vast sections of the prophetic Scriptures of the Old Testament have to do with this supreme event, while a lesser amount of the Old Testament is occupied with the events of His first advent. In the New Testament, more than three hundred times this event is mentioned, with one verse in every twenty-five promising the second coming of Christ. Since the Holy Spirit demonstrated the magnitude of this stupendous event, does it seem reasonable that any sincere Bible student could overlook its importance?

"ALL Scripture is given by the inspiration of God, and is PROFITABLE . . ." This we accept as one of the doctrines of our faith. The contemplation of our Lord's return as revealed in the Scriptures is *profitable*. And how richly this word applies to the second part of this verse (2 Tim. 3:16): ". . . profitable for doctrine, for reproof, for correction, for instruction in righteousness." And the objective stated, in verse 17, is: "That the man of God may be perfect, throughly furnished unto all good works."

3

In the light of this Scripture it is impossible for a servant of God to produce a well-rounded, balanced witness if he does not believe ALL the revealed Word of God. Obviously, this includes the eschatology of the Bible. Although all details of God's program for the future of this world may not be fully understod, yet the central doctrine of Christ's return is most explicit.

Now, this truth which Paul calls "the blessed hope" is of supreme practical value in the lives of God's people. The hope of His coming was the guiding inspiration of six million martyrs of the early generations of the church. They were glad to die for the witness of Christ because through the flaming faggots they could see the coming day of His glory when He would triumph over all His enemies.

It was the teaching of the second coming of Christ which gave depth and breadth to the preaching of those peerless leaders of the Reformation. It was Martin Luther who, in the dark days of that struggle, said: "I ardently hope that, amidst these internal dissensions on the earth, Jesus Christ will hasten the day of His coming." The brave soul of John Knox was fired by this hope. He wrote: "Has not the Lord Jesus, in despite of Satan's malice, carried up our flesh into heaven? And shall He not return? We know that He shall return, and that with expedition."

The intrepid John Wesley, pioneer of Methodism, entertained this blessed hope, as is evidenced by his commentary on the closing verses of the Revelation: "The Spirit of adoption in the bride in the heart of every true believer says, with earnest desire and expectation, 'Come, and accomplish all the words of this prophecy.'" And, in an earlier day this glorious truth became the source of exultant joy for John Milton as expressed in his sublime supplication: "Come forth out of Thy royal chambers, O Prince of all kings of the earth; take up that unlimited scepter which Thy Almighty Father hath bequeathed Thee.

For now the voice of Thy bride calleth Thee, and all creatures sigh to be renewed."

To these, and to millions of others, this hope has been intensely practical. "That blessed hope" is of priceless value, and there are many reasons why it is so:

It is an *enlightening hope*. It gives perspective. It enables us to see the march of God through the ages. It gives us a panoramic view of His program, not merely for this age, but for the ages to come. By this truth the sinner is made to realize that God intends to deal with him, and there is a day of accountability—thus he is convicted. He understands that if he yields to the Christ of Calvary and of the empty tomb, he will have no dread of the Great White Throne judgment. By this truth, believers are constantly reminded to fulfill their discipleship against that day when they shall stand before another judgment throne —the Judgment Seat of Christ.

It is a *stabilizing hope*. It gives spiritual depth to one's convictions. Intertwined with all the other doctrines of our faith, it gives assurance and purpose. Those who entertain the blessed hope do not call in question the verities of God's Word. When this doctrine is believed, all other doctrines are accepted in the simplicity of faith. The exercise of this hope, together with other doctrines, becomes the antidote against heresy, and modernism. It is a balance staff, enabling the believer to avoid impatience. "Be ye also patient: *stablish your hearts:* for the coming of the Lord draweth nigh," Jas. 5:8.

It is also a *sanctifying hope*. The contemplation of that day of all days when Christ shall come for His people will always have the effect of self-discipline and more complete consecration. The Apostle John emphasized this fact when he wrote: ". . . But we know that when He shall appear, we shall be like Him, for we shall see Him as He is. And *every man that hath this hope in him purifieth himself,* even as He is pure," I John 3:2,3.

To be like Him is the goal of every one who loves His appearing. This fact was given special accent by Paul when he wrote the Colossian Christians of this blessed hope, and coupled it with a strong admonition: "When Christ, Who is our life shall appear, then shall ye also appear with Him in glory. Mortify therefore your members which are upon the earth . . ." Col. 3:4,5. Anticipating Christ's coming, they were to "mortify"—(make dead)—the sins of the flesh; and, then, they were to "put on" the graces and virtues of Christ.

Likewise, Peter, in an exhortation concerning the return of Christ, urged the self-discipline of believers. He solemnly questioned, "What manner of persons ought ye to be in all holy conversation and godliness, looking for and hasting unto the coming of the day of God . . .?"

The entertainment of this hope will bring about our separation from the world: "The grace of God that bringeth salvation hath appeared unto all men, teaching us, that denying ungodliness and worldly lusts, we should live soberly, righteously, and godly in this present world; looking for that blessed hope, and the glorious appearing of the great God and our Saviour Jesus Christ," Tit. 2:11-13.

It is likewise a *triumphant hope*. It enables believers to overcome. Inspiration to endure bitter trials and persecutions is gained from entertaining that future day of triumph. "Think it not strange," said Peter, "concerning the fiery trial which is to try you, as though some strange thing happened unto you; but rejoice, inasmuch as ye are partakers of Christ's sufferings; that *when His glory shall be revealed*, ye may be glad with exceeding joy." Again, he assured: "That the trial of your faith, being much more precious than of gold that perisheth, though it be tried with fire, might be found unto praise and honor and glory *at the appearing of Jesus Christ*," 1 Pet. 1:7.

This hope also *inspires faithfulness*. Our Lord gave the

parable of the talents to drive home the force of this truth. The servants would be faithful in the use of their talents because they anticipated the return of their Lord. The supreme motive for their loyalty was the hope of their lord's return. To anticipate that welcome plaudit, "Well done, thou good and faithful servant," was enough to inspire them to invest all they had in the service of their coming Lord.

It is a *love-stimulating hope.* To fulfill the new commandment of our Lord, "that ye love one another," there is nothing that will more surely encourage this love of the brethren than the common bond of faith and hope. Anticipating that day of perfect brotherhood of God's children, Paul urged this important need upon the Thessalonian believers. He said: "The Lord make you to increase and abound in love one toward another, and toward all men ... to the end that He may establish your hearts unblameable in holiness before God, even our Father, *at the coming of our Lord Jesus Christ* with all His saints."

Our Lord's return is also a *comforting hope.* When our hearts are rent with grief and the clouds of sorrow gather over our souls, it is then that "the blessed hope" of our Lord's coming will dispel every shadow. When Jesus was about to leave His disciples a spell of gloom possessed them; but they were fully comforted by the Lord's promise, "*I will come again,* and receive you unto Myself."

And what a solace to the bereaved is this bright hope of the day of His coming when He shall raise from their sleeping dust the bodies of all His people. With what majestic sweetness do these words in First Thessalonians 4:13-18 ring in our hearts today:

"... for the Lord Himself shall descend from heaven with a shout, with the voice of the archangel, and with the trump of God; and the dead in Christ shall rise first: then we which are alive and remain shall be caught up together with them in the clouds, to meet the Lord in the air; and so shall we ever be with the Lord. Wherefore, *comfort* one another with these words.''

Above all, we may think of this hope as *a Christ-honoring hope*. This blessed event was uppermost in the mind of our Lord during all His teaching ministry. According to all the revelation of God's Word it is the supreme event of all eternity, and the crowning day of glory and honor to the Son of God. It is unspeakably tremendous and breath-taking in scope. It is "the day of Jesus Christ." Why should not every child of that heavenly kingdom be overwhelmed with the anticipation of that day when to our adorable Lord and Saviour shall be ascribed by all creation the honor and praise and glory of which He is so truly and everlastingly worthy!

Therefore, the entertainment of this blessed hope in the hearts of God's people places Christ in the area of our thoughts, devotion, and service in the exalted position which He deserves: in the topmost place, and at the very pinnacle of all our activities. It makes Christ the center of all, and the judgment seat of Christ the goal of the believer's life.

II Prophetic Forecast of World History

Prophetic Forecast of World History

There is no more fascinating prophetic study than the book of Daniel, written some 600 years before Christ was born at Bethlehem.

Most of us are familiar with the fantastic dream of Nebuchadnezzar, king of Babylon. He had a most terrifying dream, and like many of us, he forgot what he dreamt. He was so troubled by the awesome spectacle which he had beheld in this dream that he called for all the wise men of his empire, the astrologers, the magicians, and the sorcerers, and demanded of them, not only to interpret the dream, but, also to recall to him what the dream actually was. It was an unprecedented, a most unheard-of, request. And, of course, not a man could fulfill the king's wish.

Now, just as the king's fury was about to be unleashed toward all the wise men of his dominion—just as he had vowed to have them all put to death, Daniel, the prophet of God, stepped into the picture. Daniel reminded the king that there was "a God in heaven who revealeth secrets", and that he was able to give the king the dream and its interpretation.

It is noteworthy that Daniel, in his opening words to the king, reminded the Babylonian monarch that his dream had to do with, "What shall be in the latter days". And this is precisely where our interest centers today. We are concerned, in this series of prophetic studies, with what God's prophets have predicted for the last days of this age; and we are concerned with the question as to whether these prophecies have been, or are now being fulfilled in the times in which we live. Personally, I be-

11

lieve that there is no portion of Scripture which speaks more definitely of the end-time, or reminds us more eloquently that the coming of our Lord draws near.

To note briefly the strange and awesome dream of King Nebuchadnezzar: He beheld a colossal image of a man, with a head of gold, breasts and arms of silver, belly and thighs of brass, legs of iron, and feet of mixed iron and clay. Here was a prophetic forecast of the world's history, from Babylon to the end of this present age. The four great world kingdoms marched before him, and it is nothing short of astonishing when we mark the amazing exactitude of history as seen in this prophecy. There is no finer illustration of the axiom that prophecy is history pre-written than in this instance. The interpretation is plainly given: The head of gold represented the Babylonian kingdom under Nebuchadnezzar—"thou art this head of gold". It was a golden monarchy whose scepter controlled the great nations of the earth, and whose influence reached around the world.

But this golden kingdom was to be replaced by the kingdom of silver, as represented by the giant image in the chest and arms of silver, a description of the Medo-Persian empire. This second kingdom of world dominion continued until the year 333 BC, when under the mighty conqueror Alexander the Great, the kingdom passed to the Greeks. The Greek-Macedonian empire is represented by the belly and thighs, or haunches, of brass. This third world empire continued in full sway for about 300 years.

Then came the fourth world kingdom, the Roman Empire, represented by the legs of iron. The Eastern and the Western portions of the Roman empire are represented by the two legs. This mighty kingdom of iron was to be the last world kingdom. There would not be another. Eventually it would have a form of ten kingdoms, some strong and some weak, as represented by the mixed iron and potter's clay. This particular period looks to the very last days of man's political rule on this earth.

The entire prophecy is amazing beyond words. Looking upon history from the perspective of this 20th century, we are fascinated by the fact that world history from Daniel's day has followed exactly the pattern as outlined by the prophet in his interpretation of the meaning of the colossal image of gold, silver, brass, iron, and of mixed iron and clay.

Perhaps one of the most astonishing features of this prophecy is the declaration that the Roman kingdom would be the last—not the last of four—but the last of all, the end of man's political dominion on this earth. How could Daniel have known that no other kingdom would rise to world dominion? It would have been but the natural supposition that since the Babylonians would give way to the Medes and Persians, and they in turn would fall before the Greeks, who, in course of time would surrender their scepter to the Romans—that, at length, when the Romans ceased to dominate the world, that surely another great warrior-conqueror would rise on the horizon who would gather in his hands the reins of power, and forge a new world empire, perhaps stronger than any in previous history. (For the trend was for progressively stronger kingdoms: the gold is the softest medal; the silver is stronger than gold; the brass is stronger than silver; and the iron is stronger than brass).

But it is singularly strange that, although many attempts were made, after the decay of the Roman Empire, in the centuries that followed, to grasp the scepter of world dominion, all were to no avail. In the fifth century the savage warriors of the North poured their hordes into the mighty effort to overthrow the nations to the south and west, but all such predatory attempts spent their strength without accomplishing their goals.

In the seventh century, the Arabs made a determined effort to wrest the scepter of world rule. They marched out of the desert, attacking on the East and on the West, and it seemed for a time that they would ascend the throne of the Caesars. But they did not succeed.

The blood-thirsty Charlemagne almost succeeded, but he failed.

The mighty Napoleon Bonaparte came very close to holding the world in his grasp, but was stopped in his tracks.

In modern times, such men as Kaiser Wilhelm, and Mussolini, and Hitler have been ambitious to rule the world, but each has met with ignominious defeat.

With warfare and communications what they are today, it would seem less difficult for some bloodthirsty warlord to overcome the weaker nations, one by one, and finally rule the world.

But God has spoken. He has revealed that no such ruler will appear until Antichrist appears to rule the ten-power kingdom, which in the end-time will be a revival of the old Roman Empire. Such a superman shall rise on the horizon of time, and forge together that identical territory which was once Caesar's empire, and shall rule with a mighty hand.

Now, back to Daniel's interpretation of the king's dream. He beheld this mighty image, representing the four great world dominions, each succeeding the other, until the last—the Roman empire. Strangely, he beheld the awe-inspiring sight of a mixture of strength and weakness in the ten-power kingdom, represented by the toes of the image—"part iron and part potter's clay." This was the final form of man's political dominion on the earth—and there was to be no other.

There was to be no other because there was to be the swift destruction of the image by divine judgment. He beheld an astonishing phenomenon: a Stone, cut out without hands, "smote the image on his feet that were of iron and clay, and brake them in pieces. Then was the iron, the clay, the brass, the silver, and the gold broken to pieces together, and became like the chaff of the summer threshingfloors; and the wind carried them away: and the Stone that smote the image became a great mountain, and filled the whole earth."

And, in the interpretation, this Stone "cut out without hands," Daniel prophesied, these words concerning that future glorious kingdom of Christ: "And in the days of these kings shall the God of heaven set up a kingdom which shall never be destroyed: and the kingdom shall not be left to other people, but it shall break in pieces and consume all these kingdoms, and it shall stand forever." Then Daniel concluded his interpretation of the king's dream in these words to Nebuchadnezzar: "The great God hath made known to the king what shall come to pass hereafter . . . and the dream is certain, and the interpretation thereof is sure."

These God-inspired prophecies concerning the course of events, leading up to the establishing of Christ's kingdom, seem to point with an index finger to the fact that we are living in the very last days of this age, and we may therefore expect the coming of our Lord for His waiting people at any moment.

While we do not know exactly what the order of events shall be, it is perfectly clear from the Word of prophecy that the coming of our Lord for His people is imminent, that is, it may be at any moment. I am of the sincere opinion that the church will not be here during the great tribulation and the reign of the Antichrist. By the church, I do not mean the professing church, and all those who have their names on a church roll; I mean what the Bible describes as the true church—born-again believers, the faithful, those who are truly the members of the spiritual body of Christ, the redeemed of God, those who have been justified—not by works of their own righteousness—but by the precious blood of Christ; those who claim no basis for salvation but the atoning death of Christ; those who claim no merit but the righteousness of God through faith in Jesus Christ. (Rom. 3:22) All such, at the sound of the trumpet, will be snatched away, "caught up" to be with the Lord.

Then will follow the terrifying judgments on this earth, described so vividly in hundreds of Bible prophecies. There will be the horrible reign of the Man of Sin, the Antichrist, under whose Satanic rule a large portion of the population of the earth will be destroyed. The battle of Armageddon will be fought—the most terrifying of all wars, during which undoubtedly all the horrors of nuclear warfare will be employed. God only knows the misery of those days. At Jerusalem there will be a great crying unto God, and a great spirit of repentance. At the height and at the depth of the crisis the Son of God shall be revealed in power and great glory. The Jews shall "look on Him whom they have pierced", and shall recognize Him as their Messiah, and shall fall at His blessed feet. All who stand in His way shall be instantly destroyed. And forthwith Christ, our Lord and Saviour, and the Jews' Messiah shall establish His kingdom of peace and righteousness on this earth. And what a glorious kingdom it shall be.

This is what Daniel the prophet saw when he beheld the "Stone cut out without hands", falling on the feet of the Gentile image, and crushing it, grinding it to powder. This Stone, then, becomes a great mountain which fills all the earth. Oh, what a day that will be!

I am thankful that the day of grace is still here. God's door of opportunity is still open to all who will enter into the overtures of His mercies. My friend, have *you* entered in?

III World-Wide Rebellion and Christ's Ultimate Triumph

World-Wide Rebellion and Christ's Ultimate Triumph

> *"Why do the heathen rage, and the people imagine a vain thing? The kings of earth set themselves, and the rulers take counsel together, against the Lord, and against His Annointed, saying, Let us break their bands asunder, and cast away their cords from us,"* Psalm 2.

Mark the expression, "Why do the heathen rage?" As a world of mad men, the nations of the earth are described as being in a wild tumult against God, their Creator. The people also "imagine a vain thing," this malice against heaven is not confined to the counsel chambers of the kings, but also includes all the subjects and citizens of the nations.

This infernal scheme to dethrone the Almighty is a determined one, for it is said, "the kings of the earth *set themselves*". It is also a deliberate and carefully devised plan, for it says that they are to "take counsel together". They seem to be sure of their ground; they seem to have a confidence that they shall succeed in their enterprise. It may be that after the true church is snatched away from the earth, as the Antichrist succeeds in getting his hand on the reins of government, and as he finds that he is not to be met with any opposition from the church, that in his arrogance he shall assume that God has already been defeated in the earth, and therefore it will be but an easy matter to overthrow Him utterly from all government of the earth. Men will be so emboldened and defiant that they shall say, "Let us break their bands asunder, and cast away their cords from us".

19

This will seem to be the day of absolute triumph for the atheists. This is, in fact, the present goal of the "Four A's". (The American Association for the Advancement of Atheism), In thinking of this challenge against God, we should read of the goal of this organization which is at war against God and the Bible. Here is what they are seeking to do: From the tract which they are sending out, entitled, "War Declared Against God and the Bible— Intention of 4 A's",—listen to this challenge which comes from the bottomless pit:

"The 4 A's will undertake to abolish public chaplaincies, to tax ecclesiastical property, to repeal Sunday legislation, to abrogate ALL laws enforcing Christian morals, to stop the BOOTLEGGING OF RELIGION into the public schools, to prevent the issuance of religious proclamations by government officials, to remove the church cross from above the national flag, and to erase the superstitious inscription that defaces our coins. Its main purpose is to DECLARE WAR ON RELIGION ITSELF. We shall begin by attacking Theism, the taproot of the tree of religious superstition. THERE IS NO GOD; and our supreme effort will be to free mankind from the fear of a nonentity. The worshipping of a verbal idol must end."

As we read this diabolical pronouncement, and consider that it is issued by an organization which is operating under a charter in the state of New York, we are forced to admit that this prophecy in the 2nd Psalm is fast approaching fulfillment. "The kings of the earth set themselves, and the rulers take counsel together, against the Lord, and against His anointed, saying, Let us break their bands asunder, and cast away their cords from us." Already there are great nations that are officially declaring war on God and the Bible: such as, the Communist government of Russia.

Let us remember that early in their atheistic crusade, there appeared on the front page of a daily newspaper in

Russia a cartoon, wherein was pictured a Russian climbing a ladder which reached toward Heaven, and with a club in his hand, he was making this statement: "We have dethroned the earthly Czar, and now we will dethrone the Heavenly Czar." The conflict is now on. Hell has declared war on Heaven, and in the day of the Antichrist this war will be fought to a finish.

Now, as the Psalmist-prophet sees this challenge against God and against His Christ, he raises the question— "Why?" Why do the heathen rage, and the people imagine a vain thing? Why do rulers take counsel together against the Lord? Why do they want to cast off the yoke, and the government of God?

And well may we ponder this question also. What has the God of Heaven done that He should be so held in contempt and despised by His own creatures? Why, what evil hath He done? Has He not created all things, and does He not uphold all things by the word of His power? Has He not been a bountiful provider, has He not been rich in mercy, rich in grace, rich in blessings? Has his heart not bled for the sons of men? Has He not provided redemption for our fallen, sinful race, even at the cost of His own dear Son's sacrifice? Has He not been patient and forbearing with men in their rebellion against Him? Therefore, why, oh *why,* is there a raging, a tumult, an uprising, an enmity against God? Are men so vile that they will turn on such matchless love; are they so wretched as to despise Him who bore their own guilt to rescue them from hell?.

Yes, this is an accurate picture of the human race at its very worst: in a rage against God. "The carnal mind is enmity against God; for it is not subject to the law of God, neither indeed can be." And this is true with every unsaved soul. There is war in the heart against God and against Christ. And what is at the heart of it? It is expressed in these words, "Let us break their bands asunder, and cast away their cords from us". It is self will, nothing less than the desire to have one's own way about everything, and to have God's way about nothing. And this prophecy teaches that there is coming a time when, under the power of Antichrist, men shall be organized against God, in an attempt to utterly throw off the yoke and government of God.

Now, the Psalmist reminds us that this attempt is but a "vain thing". It will be but an empty, useless, futile undertaking. God cannot be defeated, and how absurd to suppose that the Almighty shall change His plans because of the raging vanities of an arrogant, sinful race! All the wicked counsels of men shall not disturb Him that sitteth upon the throne!

Mark that expression, "He that sitteth in the Heavens". How calm, serene, unmoved! Think of the contrast, the "raging" of the heathen, and the quiet composure of Him that "sitteth" in the Heavens. Here is marvelous comfort for the saints. When we are surrounded many times with the tumultous noises of the wicked; when we hear the name of our God blasphemed and ridiculed; when it appears for the moment that we have lost the fight for righteousness and truth; when it seems that Satan shall succeed in overturning what we have done in the name of Jesus—then, let us remember, and take courage, for our Sovereign Lord is *sitting in the Heavens!*

Now, what is God's attitude concerning this raging challenge which men are wont to hurl at Him? He that sitteth in the heavens *shall laugh*. How strange, how solemn, how awful are these words, "He shall laugh". There are times in this age when men think they have the laugh on God. There is a time coming when He shall have the laugh on them! But this laughter must not be thought of as a laughter of joy, but rather, the laughter of contempt, the laughter of scorn! He shall laugh at their calamity, He shall mock when their fear cometh. "The

Lord shall have them in derision." He shall hold them
in holy contempt. They shall be utterly despised, since
they have become so utterly base, and hopelessly void of
gratitude, and so thoroughly engulfed in wickedness. Oh,
it will be a fearful thing for sinners to stand before God
in that awful day when mercy shall be no more, and when
grace shall be withdrawn from the earth! "He that
sitteth in the Heavens shall laugh." "The Lord shall
have them in derision".

"Then shall He speak unto them in His wrath, and vex
them in His sore displeasure." Now the Lord becomes
active. No longer is He seen sitting still. The cup of iniquity is full. The hour for the exercise of God's holy
vengeance has come. And what an awful day it shall be for
this old world!

"Then shall He speak unto them in His wrath . . ."
What terrifying words are these! Strange words to many
who do not understand the character of God! Many there
are who prefer to think of God as a one-sided Being—all
love and mercy, and no wrath or judgment.

Men need to be reminded of the fact that our God is
a God of holiness, and He therefore hates sin; and that as
a God of justice, He must punish sin. It is only because
of His boundless mercy that He *delays* punishment of
those who break, and desecrate, and trample under foot
His holy laws. God pleads with the sinner through the
Gospel to repent, and declares that He is "not willing that
any should perish, but that all should come to repentance".

But there is coming a day when God's patience and
forebearance shall be overtaxed. At that time His overtures of mercy toward the sinner shall be withdrawn. The
flaming, consuming fire of His wrath shall be revealed
toward all sin. The white heat of divine justice shall move
the Almighty One in the exercise of wrath and fiery indignation.

At that time all creation shall bow before Him in acknowledging His just judgments—they shall bow, not in repentance, but in the full admission of guilt. "Every knee shall bow, of things in heaven, and things on the earth, and things under the earth; and every tongue shall confess that Christ is Lord to the glory of God the Father." This means that every Christ-rejector, as well as all the saints of God, shall confess the Lordship of Christ; but, alas, it will be the confession of a sinner who accepts the just judgment of Almighty God.

What fearful words are these, "Then shall He speak unto them in His wrath, and vex them in His sore displeasure". When Christ comes the second time, it shall not be as it was on His first advent.

He came the first time to die in the sinner's place. He is coming the second time to execute judgment on the sinner.

He came the first time to seek and to save that which was lost. He is coming the second time "in flaming fire to execute judgment on all them that know not God".

He came the first time to be man's representative before a God of love and grace. He is coming the second time as God's representative against a rebellious world.

He came the first time in great humility; He is coming the second time in great power and glory.

He came the first time as the lowly Nazarene; He is coming the second time as the King of Kings and Lord of Lords.

He came the first time to wear the crown of thorns; He is coming the second time to wear the crown of glory.

He came the first time to be "despised and rejected of men". He is coming the second time to be acknowledged by all, both high and low, rich and poor, bond and free.

He came the first time to ride the lowly ass into Jerusalem. He is coming the second time to ride the great white horse, leading the armies of Heaven.

He came the first time to submit to the unjust judgment of earthly potentates. He is coming the second time to compel all earthly rulers to yield their scepters to Him.

He came the first time to shed His blood on the cross. He is coming again as the mighty Conqueror whose "vesture is dipped in blood".

He came the first time to save men from a devil's hell. He comes the second time to say to all the workers of iniquity, "Depart ye, into everlasting fire, prepared for the devil and his angels".

Yes, the wrath of God is to be revealed from heaven. Oh, pause, I beg that you pause, and weigh the eternal weight of these words, "Then shall He speak unto them in His WRATH, and vex them in HIS SORE DISPLEASURE".

This is the day that the prophet Zephaniah saw, when he said, "The great day of the Lord is near, it is near, and hasteth greatly, even the voice of the day of the Lord: the mighty man shall cry there bitterly. That day is a day of wrath, a day of trouble and distress, a day of wasteness and desolation, a day of darkness and gloominess, a day of clouds and thick darkness, a day of the trumpet and alarm against the fenced cities, and against the high towers. And I will bring distress upon men, that they shall walk like blind men, because they have sinned against the Lord: and their blood shall be poured out as dust, and their flesh as the dung. Neither their silver nor their gold shall be able to deliver them in the day of the Lord's wrath; but the whole land shall be devoured by the fire of His jealousy: for He shall make even a speedy riddance of all them that dwell in the land," (Zeph. 1:14-18).

This is the awful day spoken of in the first chapter of 2nd Thessalonians, where we read that "the Lord Jesus shall be revealed from Heaven with His mighty angels, in flaming fire taking vengeance on them that know not God, and that obey not the Gospel of our Lord Jesus Christ: who shall be punished with everlasting destruction from the presence of the Lord and from the glory of His power''.

Yes, the Psalmist says, ''He shall speak unto them in His wrath, and vex them in His sore displeasure''. And, mark the next statement: ''Yet have I set My King upon My holy hill of Zion.'' Ah, there is Christ now seated on the earth! The battle of Armageddon is ended, and Christ is establishing His throne on the earth!

The prophet Zechariah also saw the whole picture:

> ''Behold, the day of the Lord cometh, and thy spoil shall be divided in the midst of thee. For I will gather all nations against Jerusalem to battle; and the city shall be taken, and the houses rifled, and the women ravished; and half of the city shall go forth into captivity, and the residue of the people shall not be cut off from the city. Then shall the Lord go forth, and fight against those nations, as when He fought in the days of battle. And His feet shall stand in that day upon the mount of Olives,'' (Zech. 14:1-4).

Now, in this Psalm, we have listened to the raging, tumultuous, defiant rebellion of the human race against God; and next we have heard the solemn fearful reply of Him that sitteth in the Heavens: it is the statement of God the Father. Now, let us listen to the majestic words of God the Son. Hear Him as He says: ''I will declare the decree: the Lord hath said unto Me, Thou art My Son, this day have I begotten Thee.''

All authority and power is given unto Him both in Heaven and in earth. Seated on His throne in Jerusalem He shall declare the decree of the Father. Now, He speaks further: ''Ask of Me, and I shall give thee the heathen for Thine inheritance, and the uttermost parts of the earth for Thy possession.'' Ah, this is the promise

which God the Father has made to God the Son; this is
the everlasting covenant. The heathen, or the nations,
shall be His inheritance; and the uttermost parts of the
earth shall be His possession. His millennial kingdom shall
be earthwide, and the knowledge of the Lord shall cover
the earth as the waters that cover the sea.

IV The Execution of God's Wrath on the Earth

The Execution of God's Wrath on the Earth

"It is a fearful thing to fall into the hands of the living God," (Heb. 10:31).

There are some good people who have conceived of the idea that the God of this universe is a Person of *all love and mercy*. They do not want to think of Him as One who would punish individuals or nations. They do not want to think of Him as a God of judgment. They do not want to think of Him as One who is capable of administering a fiery retribution on those who trample under foot His holy laws.

To these people God is a one-sided Being—a God of pure love and goodness, and not a God of wrath. Now, just think of this for a moment: If He were such a Person, He would be a God without character. Our God is a God of Holiness who hates sin. He is a God of Justice, whose very nature demands that He must punish sin.

It must be quite convenient, and soothing to one's conscience, to have a God who will always overlook sin, and who will never punish the sinner. But such a God could only exist in the figment of the imagination of a deluded soul. Such a God could never be a reality, because we all know that sin is a reality; and a God who is holy and righteous would never condone that which is so totally antagonistic to His nature and will. Sin is a force that God Almighty must deal with. There must be judgment and retribution against all that is evil in God's Universe.

We must remember that this is God's Universe, and whatever interferes with His design and purpose is an

29

offense unto Him. Sin is an abomination to God. He hates it with a holy hatred. And because He is a just God, He must punish sin.

The kind of God we have revealed in the holy Scriptures is a God of both love and judgment. He is not a nebulous nonentity of sentimentalism. He is a God of character. We thank God today that He is a God of love and mercy—and there would not be one of us alive today to breathe His fresh air, if it were not for His amazing love toward us. For we, as sinful creatures, do not deserve anything at the hand of God whose laws we have transgressed. If we had received our just deserts, we would have been stamped out of existence long ago.

Yes, God loves us, and as proof of this, Christ died for us. The greatest proof that hell is a reality is the fact that the Son of God went to the cross to die in the sinner's place. Only divine love could provide such a redemption as that. The God whose we are is a God of fiery indignation against sin. Most solemnly, He caused the prophet to write down the verdict: "The soul that sinneth, it shall die." There is therefore no hope for the sinner if it is not to be found in the sacrifice for sin which Christ has made. Thank God, there is everlasting hope in the crucified and risen Son of God. "For God so loved the world, that He gave His only begotten Son, that whosoever believeth in Him should not perish, but have everlasting life," (John 3:16).

Those who do not want to believe that God will administer justice in respect to sin, should be reminded that the Bible reveals that God is exactly that kind of a Being. In the very cradle of human history, we find God pronouncing a curse upon our first parents on account of their transgression. He even pronounced a curse on the earth itself on account of their sin.

After a while, when sin abounded in the earth, in that antedeluvian era, we find God executing judgment on the whole human race in the dreadful flood which destroyed all flesh, except for Noah and his family who "found grace in the eyes of the Lord".

Upon the wicked nation of Egypt, God sent not one, but ten, of the most severe judgments of which only divine justice could conceive and execute.

Upon the wicked, idolatrous nations of Canaan, God caused the judgment of war to fall, which wiped out twenty-odd kingdoms in one sweeping purge.

Upon the proud Assyrians, God sent destruction because of their sins.

Upon the haughty Babylonian Empire God spoke in thunderous tones of judgment, and by the handwriting on the wall of the palace of King Belshazzar, the first neon sign blazed the fearful doom of that idolatrous kingdom in these words: "THOU ART WEIGHED IN THE BALANCES AND FOUND WANTING."

And in like manner, God sent His judgment of destruction upon the Medo-Persian empire; and later, the Greeco-Macedonian kingdom; and later still, upon that kingdom of iron, the mighty Roman Empire. Because of their sins, they were destroyed.

Nor did God spare His own chosen people, the Israelites. Because of their unbelief and idolatry, and witchcraft, and rebellion, and haughtiness of spirit, God sent upon them the judgment of the captivities. Nor has any nation ever been spared to live which has stubbornly transgressed God's holy laws. "Vengeance is mine: I will repay, saith the Lord." . . . "It is a fearful thing to fall into the hands of the living God." If you believe history, you must believe that God is a God of judgment.

There is nothing more clearly or more solemnly taught in the Word of God than that teaching of a final judgment of a grim and fiery retribution on all the wicked, a day of judgment in which this earth will catch on fire, and melt with fervent heat, and be utterly destroyed. With what

God's method will be in executing such a cataclysmic judgment on this earth, we have never been particularly concerned. We know that a God who is all powerful, who is able to make a world like this, is able also to destroy it. And while it is not necessarily important that you and I know just what method the Almighty will employ in this final judgment, it is, nevertheless, highly significant that in the light of many, many Scriptures which speak of this judgment, we have disclosed all of the horrible characteristics of the atom bomb which has so lately been introduced into the world.

Writing under the inspiration of the Spirit of God, the Apostle Peter said, concerning that day: "The day of the Lord will come as a thief in the night, in which the heavens shall pass away with a great noise, and the elements shall melt with fervent heat, and the earth also and the works that are therein shall be burned up," (2 Peter 3:10).

The occasion for these solemn words by Peter was the complaint that some scoffers were making concerning the promised return of Christ to the earth. Peter told them that the reason for the delay in Christ's return to earth was the longsuffering of God in seeking men through the Gospel to repent and to be saved, and to escape the damnation of the forthcoming judgment. He said, "The Lord is not slack concerning His promise, as some men count slackness; but is longsuffering toward us, not willing that any should perish, but that all should come to repentance."

Having given this word of assurance, he then proceeds to describe the terrible earth-wide cataclysmic judgment which would come in God's appointed time. He therefore warns of that day when "the earth shall be burned up," and also "the heavens shall pass away with a great noise" (that is, the firmament, or the asmospheric heavens. not the stellar heavens). All of this should be read in· connection with the 20th and 21st chapters of Revelation in which John was shown the same picture. After seeing the terrific judgments which were to be sent on all the earth, he was also given to see the "new heavens and the new earth". He said, "And I saw a new heaven and a new earth: for the first heaven and the first earth were passed away".

It is well that we note with a new emphasis, some of the many Scriptures which speak of that final day of God's righteous judgment of this earth and its wicked inhabitants.

In Psalm 9:17, we read: "The wicked shall be turned into hell, and all the nations that forget God."

In Hebrews 9:27, we read, "It is appointed unto men once to die, but after this the judgment."

In Acts 17:31, we read, "He hath appointed a day in which He will judge the world by that man whom He hath ordained".

The Prophet Joel saw this dreadful day through the telescope of divine revelation. He cried out, "Blow ye the trumpet in Zion, and sound an alarm in my holy mountain: let all the inhabitants of the land tremble: for the day of the Lord cometh, for it is nigh at hand; a day of darkness and gloominess a day of clouds and thick darkness, as the morning spread upon the mountains . . . a fire devoureth before them; and behind them a flame burneth: the land is as the Garden of Eden before them, and behind them a desolate wilderness; yea, and nothing shall escape them . . . before their face the people shall be much pained: all faces shall gather blackness". (Think of that statement in the light of the atom bomb).

Likewise, the Prophet Isaiah was given to see these things. He exclaimed: "Lift up your eyes to the heavens, and look upon the earth beneath; for the heavens shall vanish away like smoke, and the earth shall wax old like a garment, and they that dwell therein shall die in like manner," (Isa. 51.6).

David the Psalmist was given to see this world judgment. We read in Psalm 50:1, 3-6: "The mighty God, even the Lord, hath spoken, and called the earth from the rising of the sun unto the going down thereof . . . our God shall come and shall not keep silence: a fire shall devour before Him, and it shall be very tempestuous round about Him. He shall call to the heavens from above, and to the earth, that He may judge His people. Gather My saints together unto Me; those that have made a covenant with Me by sacrifice. And the heavens shall declare His righteousness, for God is judge Himself."

Likewise, the Prophet Daniel had a vision of this terrible day of judgment. He said: "I beheld till the thrones were cast down, and the Ancient of days did sit, whose garment was white as snow, and the hair of His head like the pure wool: His throne was like the fiery flame, and His wheels as burning flame. A fiery stream issued and came forth from before Him: thousand thousands ministered unto Him, and ten thousand times ten thousand stood before Him: the judgment was set, and the books were opened."

Now, coming back for a final glance at this prophecy of Peter. He says these judgments shall be accompanied "with a great noise". It will be a terrible blast that shall be heard by every living soul. It shall shake the earth with a mighty tremor. The deep-toned thunder of the Almighty shall roll out with such a deafening sound that all the world will know what is taking place. It will be the sound of an atomic bomb multiplied ten-thousandfold, or by one million, or even a billion times the force by which it can be produced by human hands.

Mark well these words, "the elements shall melt with fervent heat". Scientists say that the atom bomb dropped on Hiroshima generated a heat of some two trillion degrees centigrade—a heat utterly incomprehensible to the human mind. "A FERVENT HEAT." All life was literally seared out of existence! Human beings were burned beyond all identity! The devastation wrought will never be described, because no human language can begin to explain it!

Another word we must not overlook: the word "melt"— the elements shall MELT. This is the actual effect of the atom bomb: In addition to the terrific blast from without, there is the explosion simultaneously of millions of atoms which dissolve into gases, and in turn the gases explode, affecting all the elements within a radius of miles.

If man, in his finite capacity, can devise a bomb from the tiny, microscopic atoms from the element of Uranium 235, sufficient in power to blast out of existence an entire city, how could anyone ever doubt the ability of the omnipotent and infinite God who created the heavens and the earth to produce in a single second an atomic explosion which could melt with fervent heat the elements of the entire world, just as He declared through the inspired prophets and apostles that He will do!

But it is not necessary for any man to perish in that dreadful final judgment, because God, in infinite mercy, has provided a remedy. He is "not willing that any should perish, but that all should come to repentance," (2 Peter 3:9).

"For God so loved the world that He gave His only begotten Son, that whosoever believeth in Him should not perish, but have everlasting life. For God sent not His Son into the world to condemn the world; but that the world through Him might be saved," (John 3:16, 17).

V Perspective of the End-Time

Perspective of the End-Time

A perspective of the last days is most important. Why are these dreadful judgments to be executed by the God who "so loved the world that He gave His only begotten Son, that whosoever believeth on Him should not perish, but have everlasting life"? When are these judgments to commence? How long are they to last? What peoples of the world will be affected by them? What is God's revealed objective in the consummation of this age?

We must bear in mind the fact that these fearsome judgments which we have reviewed are long overdue. God has, because of His infinite mercy, *delayed* the execution of His wrath on this rebellious world. Because He is "not willing that any should perish, but that all should come to repentance", He has exercised unspeakable forebearance and patience, giving generation after generation an opportunity to repent.

He has also been patient with His church, to which He gave the Great Commission to "preach the Gospel to every creature". The church should have long ago evangelized the world, but she has been slothful, neglectful, indifferent to the call of dying men. But God has been patient and long-suffering.

But the cup of iniquity is now full, to the brim, and as a just God, He must execute a fiery retribution. For "the Lord Jesus Christ shall be revealed from heaven with His mighty angels, in flaming fire taking vengeance on them that know not God, and that obey not the Gospel of our Lord Jesus Christ; who shall be punished with everlasting destruction from the presence of the Lord, and from the

glory of His power; when He shall come to be glorified in
His saints, and to be admired in all them that believe . . .
in that day," (2 Thess. 1:7-10).   Remember, at that day
the door of mercy will be closed, and the day of grace shall
be over.

Now, that great and terrible day, which is described as
"the day of the Lord" in many, many prophecies, is a
definite time-period. All of these horrible events, includ-
ing the Great Tribulation and the Battle of Armageddon
shall occur within a time period of some seven years. Let
us turn to the 8th and 9th chapters of the book of Daniel.

The prophet Daniel was given a dream. It was a dream
of a ram and a billy goat. Unfolded in that dream was
the coming Antichrist, the man of sin, and the horrible
tortures he should inflict on the Jews at Jerusalem in the
last days. These same atrocities were later described by
Jesus in the 24th chapter of Matthew. This Man of Sin
is to desecrate the temple at Jerusalem, in a sin which is
described both by Daniel and Jesus as "the abomination
of desolation".

These revelations caused Daniel to have great distress
of spirit. He was so heavily burdened that he fainted,
and became very ill. Subsequently, he fasted and went
into a prolonged period of supplication, confessing his
sins, and the sins of his nation, Israel. At this point, the
angel Gabriel appeared to him, and revealed God's pattern
respecting Israel, and the time period which was to be
allotted them. The length of time was described as "seventy weeks". Literally, seventy sevens of years, or a total
of 490 years. This period began, the angel said, at the
commandment of king Artaxerxes to return and rebuild
Jerusalem. The angel said that 69 of these 70 weeks would
be fulfilled, and then "Messiah would be cut off". It was
exactly sixty-nine weeks of years, or 483 years from that
named date in history until the Lord Jesus Christ, Israel's
Messiah, was crucified in Jerusalem.

Afterward, there would be another seven years, but this was to be delayed for an indefinite period of time. It would occur at the end of the age, and coincident with the reign of Antichrist. The angel Gabriel declared that this prince of the Gentiles would enter into a covenant with the Jews at Jerusalem, but that "in the midst of the week" he would violate it, and completely disregard it. That definitive expression, "in the midst of the week" means literally "at the middle of the week" is made clear by the statement in Daniel 12:7: "a time, times, and a half"— that is "a year, years, and a half-year". And again is mentioned the period as twelve hundred and sixty days, which is three and one-half years. Again in Revelation 13:5 this period is described as "forty and two months".

So the blasphemous reign of the Antichrist is to reach over that seven-year period.

Now, just how long is the time period between the end of the sixty-ninth week (the 483 years) and the beginning of the 70th week (the final seven years) is indeterminate. It was not given the Prophet Daniel, or any of the other Old Testament prophets to see or understand the period which we know as the church age. When the church age has ended by the rapture of born-again believers, that final seven-year period shall commence. At the end of Daniel's 70th week "the times of the Gentiles" is brought to a close, and Israel, God's chosen nation, after continuing in unbelief for so many centuries, and after having been punished so severely in the Great Tribulation and the Battle of Armageddon, shall cry out to God in great distress, and shall repent when they see their Messiah coming through the clouds in great power and glory. At that moment they shall recognize Him as the Jesus of Nazareth whom they crucified, and shall know that He is indeed their Messiah, for "they shall look on Him whom they have pierced".

Now, I do not understand from the prophetic Scriptures that every member of the Israelitish nation shall be converted in that day, but the Scriptures do declare that "a nation shall be born in a day". This could well mean the nation representatively, all the tribes, but not necessarily every individual Jew.

But this event shall be the highest mountain peak in the history of Israel, the recognition and owning of their Messiah. It shall be wonderful, beyond words, to see the display of the unspeakable mercy and the indescribable grace of God toward this wayward Nation, so long in unbelief; so long in rebellion and open rejection of Christ.

As those tremendous events move toward a climax, and toward the grand finale in this drama of God, we behold the Judge of all the earth executing justice on the Antichrist, and the false prophet, and the nations of the world, arrayed in war against God. The fearful retribution then begins, and the fiery indignation of an offended God shall execute judgment on the nations without one iota of mercy.

It shall be the fearful time described in the 6th chapter of Revelation, in these words:

"And I beheld when He opened the sixth seal, and lo, there was a great earthquake; and the sun became black as sackcloth of hair, and the moon became as blood; and the stars of heaven fell unto the earth, even as a fig tree casteth her untimely figs when she is shaken of a mighty wind. And the heaven departed as a scroll when it is rolled together; and every mountain and island were moved out of their places. And the kings of the earth, and the great men, and the rich men, and the chief captains, and the mighty men, and every bondman and every free man, hid themselves in the dens and in the rocks of the mountains; and said to the mountains and rocks, Fall on us, and hide us from the face of Him that sitteth on the throne,

and from the wrath of the Lamb: for the great day of
His wrath is come, and who shall be able to stand?''
(Rev. 6:12-17).

But let us turn our faces from that dreadful scene, and
be reminded that the redeemed of God, all those who are
washed by the blood of the Lamb, the church which is the
Bride of Christ, composed of all born-again Christians,
shall not be on the earth at that time to be baptized in
that sea of blood. They shall not be under the frown of
Almighty God, but at that very hour already have been
snatched away in the blessed Rapture, even before the
time of the Great Tribulation. Listen to the promise of
Christ to His people: ''Because thou hast kept the word
of My patience, I also will keep thee from the hour of
temptation, which shall come upon all the world, to try
them that dwell upon the earth. Behold, I come quickly;
hold that fast which thou hast, that no man take thy crown''
(Rev. 3:10, 11).

It must be emphasized that the only reason why Christians shall not be in that awful judgment is because their
sins were judged on the cross of Christ. Once on the
brow of Golgotha, the Son of God assumed our guilt, and
went to the cross to bear the penalty, to suffer the death
that we each deserved to suffer. ''He was wounded for
our transgressions; He was bruised for our iniquities; the
chastisement of our peace was upon Him; and by His
stripes we are healed.'' When in that mighty hour the
blessed Saviour bore our sins in His own body, the fiery
indignation of God was upon Him; the earth quaked and
trembled, the sun ceased to shine; and the face of God was
turned away from the earth, and away from His only
begotten Son; so that our dying Redeemer cried out, ''My
God, My God, why hast Thou forsaken Me?'' God did not
look back on this earth, and the sun did not shine again
until after God the Son had suffered the agonies of hell,
and had died for our sins!

And now it is revealed, beloved, as a glorious fact, our sins have already been judged on the cross, and God acquits every sinner who believes on the crucified and risen Saviour; and justifies every soul who rests solely under the redeeming blood. For as Jesus said, in John 5:24: "Verily, verily, I say unto you, he that heareth My word, and believeth on Him that sent Me *hath* everlasting life and shall not come into the judgment, but is passed from death unto life." And, as the Apostle expressed it, "There is therefore now no condemnation (judgment) to them which are in Christ Jesus." "Therefore, being justified by faith, we have peace with God through our Lord Jesus Christ."

I remind you—you who have not yet entered into the ark of safety; you who have not yet come to the cross—that God loves you, and is ready to receive you. Rejoice today and thank God that you have not entered that dreadful day of world judgment, but that we are yet in the day of grace—although it may well be very near the twilight of the day—and God is ready to accept you when you come to His Son for pardon, and peace, and eternal life. Trust Him now, and be saved forever!

VI   The Jew—Time Clock of History

The Jew—Time Clock of History

The history of the race, the present destiny of the nations, and the future hope of the world is inseparably linked with the nation of Israel. For one to fail to understand this is but an evidence that he is not familiar with God's prophetic Word.

For more than four thousand years the Jew has been the political wonder of the world. Their history has been so peculiarly different from that of other nations of the earth that the world has been unable to understand the sons of Abraham. But God chose this nation to be different. They were to occupy a distinct and far-reaching purpose in His program for this world. They were to represent Him to all the nations of the earth; they were to receive, preserve, and transmit the sacred Scriptures, they were to produce, (as to His humanity), the Messiah, the Saviour of the world; and, through their kingdom, with Christ on David's throne, they were to rule the world in righteousness and peace. These purposes we know have been fulfilled only in part.

We are familiar with God's gracious providence over this nation, from the time of their deliverance out of Egypt down through the centuries. Upon no other nation of the earth did God bestow such bountiful blessings, or make such gracious provision for their welfare. They were given the most well favored land in the whole inhabited earth; to them were given the oracles of God, and they were therefore vested with a superior knowledge to that possessed by other nations; and to them was revealed God's plan of redemption, and also all matters

45

pertaining to their conduct in life. Moreover, to them
was given the greatest system of political laws ever bequeathed to a nation. These things together with the
important fact that God had promised them His own
abiding presence with them, conditioned only upon their
obedience to His divine will. They were to enjoy material
prosperity, physical health, peace in the land, victory
over their enemies, and unlimited spiritual blessings. "And
I will walk among you, and will be your God, and ye shall
be My people" (Lev. 26:12).

But, on the other hand, should they wilfully turn aside
from God's statutes, and fail to heed His commandments,
they were warned of the certain Judgment that would
rest upon them, and of the unspeakable terrors that they
should suffer, (Lev. 26:14-38.) Looking through the prophetic telescope the prophets, beginning with Moses, beheld the strange future for God's chosen nation. Many
of these prophecies have now become history; many
others yet await fulfillment.

As an illustration of the hopelessly depraved condition
of humanity, this nation, this chosen nation of Israel upon
which Jehovah's heart was set, and to which His abundant
favors were given, and His marvelous forbearance and
patience was shown, these His covenant people FAILED
Him. There was not a statute they did not violate, and
not an ordinance they did not desecrate. But God, who
is rich in mercy, was not swift to execute His judgments
upon them. For their own sakes He often chastised them
in order to bring them back into His will, but they repented
not. Times without number He sent His prophets to them
to warn them of their inevitable punishment, but they did
not return to Him. The dark history of Israel's failure
to harken to God's word reached a sad climax in their
rejection of God's Son, their Messiah. "He came unto
His own, and His own received Him not."

They spit upon Him; they blasphemed His holy name; they pressed a crown of thorns upon His precious brow, and they crucified Him between two thieves. But the rejection of their Messiah was predicted. Listen to the word of Isaiah, written seven hundred years before the sacred blood of Christ stained the soil of Calvary:

"Who hath believed our report? and to whom is the arm of the Lord revealed? For He shall grow up before Him as a tender plant, and as a root out of dry ground: He hath no form nor comeliness; and when we shall see Him, there is no beauty that we should desire Him. HE IS DESPISED AND RE-JECTED OF MEN, a man of sorrows and acquainted with grief, and we hid as it were our faces from Him; He was despised, and we esteemed Him not", (Isa. 53:1-3).

David also saw this rejection of Christ one thousand years before it occurred, and he said, "The Stone which the builders rejected, the same has become the head of the corner," (Ps. 118:22).

That this rejection of Christ was to continue over a long period of time was also clearly foreseen by the prophets:

"Go, and tell this people (Israel), Hear ye indeed, but understand not; and see ye indeed, but perceive not. Make the heart of this people fat, and make their eyes heavy, and shut their eyes; lest they see with their eyes, and hear with their ears, and understand with their heart, and convert, and be healed. Then said I, Lord, how long? And He answered, UNTIL THE CITIES BE WASTED WITHOUT INHABITANT, AND THE HOUSES WITHOUT MAN, AND THE LAND BE UTTERLY DESO-LATE, AND THE LORD HAVE REMOVED MEN FAR AWAY, AND THERE BE A GREAT FOR-

SAKING IN THE MIDST OF THE LAND", (Isa. 6:9-12).

Just how long this failure to accept the claims of Christ is to continue is also made known in Romans 11:25: "Blindness in part is happened to Israel, until the fullness of the Gentiles be come in." And we know that it is God's purpose in this age to "Visit the Gentiles, to take out of them a people for His name", (Acts 15:14).

The great punishment which this chosen nation, Israel, must suffer because of her sin, and how that God should make of this nation an object lesson to all the world as to the terrible character of His judgments, was clearly foretold by God's prophets. This punishment was to be meted out to them by the sword, by famine, by captivities, by the perpetual hatred of the other nations, by the destruction of Jerusalem, by the utter desolation of the land, by exiles, and by nameless horrors which they were to suffer through the centuries. (Read Deut. 28:15-68.)

Even the nation that should accomplish this was mentioned by the prophet: "The Lord shall bring a nation against thee from afar, from the end of the earth, as swift as the eagle flieth; a nation whose tongue thou shalt not understand; a nation of fierce countenance", (Deut. 28: 49, 50). This description which exactly fits the Romans was foretold thirteen hundred years before the Roman nation came into power. Here is one of the marvels of prophecy, and one of the surest marks of the divine character of this prophecy. If this warning to Israel had been of human wisdom, it should have been the most natural thing that the writer would have threatened Israel either with a return to Egyptian bondage, or else with their overthrow by some of their dreaded enemies along the border of Palestine. But the prophet looks across the centuries to behold a nation from afar, which would accomplish their destruction at the striking of God's time clock of judgment. The Roman nation exactly fulfilled this prediction.

This nation from afar would also be heartless, cruel, and merciless in the execution of this judgment on them. A nation of fierce countenance which shall not regard the person of the old, nor show favor to the young: "And he shall eat of the fruit of thy land, and the fruit of thy cattle until thou be destroyed", (vs. 51). The awful record of the atrocities committed by the Romans on the Jews would fill many volumes.

The word of prophecy also declared that many of the Jews should be taken back to Egypt in ships, and there sold as slaves. (vs. 68.) After the Romans' great slaughter of the Jews in Jerusalem, all those who were left above 17 years of age were transported to the Egyptian mines, where all the prisoners were kept at work day and night, without intermission or rest, until they fell dead of exhaustion. The awful record of this as reported by Diodorus is indeed pathetic. He wrote: "The vast numbers employed in these mines are bound in fetters and compelled to work day and night, without intermission, and without the least hope of escape. No attention is paid to their persons; they have not even a piece of rag to cover themselves; and so wretched is their condition that every one who witnesses it deplores the excessive misery they endure. No rest, either to the sick or maimed; neither the weakness of age, nor woman's infirmities are regarded; all are driven to their work with lash, till, at last, overcome with the intolerable weight of their afflictions, they die in the midst of their toil." It was a far more terrible bondage than that from which God had freed their fathers. Multitudes were sold as slaves. According to Josephus, 97,000 were carried away from Jerusalem alone. They were dispensed with in every manner possible as so many cattle.

Verses 53 to 57 of this same prophecy describe the terrible famine that should accompany their destruction in the land, and here it is foretold that they would be forced "to eat the fruit of thine own body". According to reliable historians, such as Josephus, these very predictions were literally fulfilled.

The decimation of the Jews was also clearly marked. "And ye shall be left few in number, whereas ye were as the stars of heaven for multitude; because thou shouldst not obey the voice of the Lord thy God." (62.) According to Josephus, in the horrible massacre of Jerusalem under Titus, over 1,300,000 were actually slain, and over 101,000 were carried away as captives. And this includes only Jerusalem and two other places. The vast numbers throughout all the provinces who were slain were not even counted, and it is impossible to estimate. But this was only the beginning, for as time went on, the Jews who were left undertook from time to time to revolt, and multitudes perished in these insurrections. The worst of these insurrections was under Barochebas, and it is said that more were slain in this war than escaped with Moses from Egypt. The whole of Judea was reduced to a desert and a desolation.

The prophet also declared that they should be driven from their own land. "Ye shall be plucked from off the land whither thou goest in to possess it", (vs 63.) From the time of the emperor Hadrian until recent years, they were never permitted to call that land their own.

And we next note that their dispersion was to be universal in scope. "And the Lord shall scatter thee among all peoples from one end of the earth even to the other end of the earth." (vs 64.) "And you will I scatter among the nations." (Lev. 26:33.) The literal fulfillment of this prophecy is a matter of common knowledge. Jews are everywhere to be found on the eastern and western hemispheres. Indeed there is not a nation in the world where they are not to be found. And this fact could not apply to any other nation of people on the earth.

But the marvel of the prophetic word increases into amazement when we note, further, that, even though scattered among the nations, the Jews would be preserved. Hear the word of God: "And yet, for all that, when they be in the land of their enemies, I will not reject them, neither will I abhor them, to destroy them utterly, and to break my covenant with them; for I am the Lord their God." (Lev. 26:44.) Here is the political miracle of all time. That a nation should be scattered among all the other nations is indeed a wonder, but how could that nation survive, preserve its racial identity over nineteen hundred years, and continue without any central rallying place, and without the religious and political institutions of a fatherland? In every other instance in the history of the world, the uprooting of a nation, and its dispersion into other countries, resulted in its extinction. But not so with God's chosen nation. And there can be but one answer, it is GOD'S PURPOSE that it should be so.

And, how this nation could remain SEPARATE from all the other nations through the centuries is a marvel not to be explained on human grounds. This, however, was also predicted. "That which cometh into your mind shall not be at all; in that ye say, we will be as the nations, as the families of the countries to serve wood and stone." (Ezek. 20:32.) This prophecy indicates clearly that it has not always been the desire of the Jews to remain separate. There were times in their history when they thought it would be good policy to amalgamate with other nations, but God prevented it. How a nation may retain its national characteristics for awhile, even though dispersed, might be understood, but how these Israelites scattered among the nations of the earth, enslaved, dispirited, persecuted with relentless hatred, have succeeded in overcoming every opposing influence, and have retained their distinctive character as a nation, is indeed a divine miracle.

Added yet to this was the prediction that they should "have no rest". "Among those nations shalt thou find no ease, and there shall be no rest for the sole of thy foot; but the Lord shall give thee there a trembling heart, and failing of eyes, and pining of soul: And thy life shall hang in doubt before thee; and thou shalt fear night and day, and shalt have none assurance of thy life: In the morning thou shalt say, would God it were even! and at even thou shalt say, would God it were morning! for the fear of thine heart which thou shalt fear, and for the sight of thine eyes which thou shalt see." (Deut. 28:65-67.)

The manner in which these prophecies have been fulfilled, and are yet being fulfilled today, is one of the saddest stories in all human history. The persecutions which the nation of Israel have suffered would have been enough under any other circumstances to have completely annihilated any nation. It would require a long while to give even the barest outline of this grewsome picture of the Jews: persecutions in practically all the nations of the world, and in every century, and in every single generation since Christ was crucified. And we are all familiar with the present persecutions of the Jews. And there is no hope for the Jew that this persecution shall be discontinued in this present age. GOD SAID IT, and therefore it must continue, "until the times of the Gentiles be fulfilled".

The Prophet Hosea declared that Israel should "continue without a sacrifice and without a pillar, without an ephod and without teraphim" (Hos. 3:4, 5). Thus the very foundation of their religious institutions were to be taken from them: No temple, no sacrifice, no priestly ministration". They have replaced the priesthood with the office of the Rabbi, and continue to maintain a form of service in their synagogues. But it is all to no avail, for God cannot be approached except through Christ, "For there is one God, and one Mediator between God and men, the Man Christ Jesus".

Indeed it is a pathetic story the prophets have fore-told, and the historians have recorded, concerning this chosen, favored nation of God. Why, oh why, these terrible and long continued judgments? There can be but one answer—Israel rejected their Messiah! The very nation that should have been prepared for His coming, and eagerly welcoming His glorious redemptive work, in the accomplishment of which scores of Old Testament prophecies were fulfilled, alas, lifted up their heel against Him, rejected Him, despised Him, and crucified Him! They were the fig tree, on which, when the Master came, He found no fruit, and therefore pronounced the curse upon it.

A dark picture, yes. But wait, we are not through. We have yet a bright picture to present of this selfsame nation. These black clouds of judgment have a bright silver lining. There is a better day coming for Israel, a glorious day. These prophecies reveal that they would be re-stored to their own land, and what is more, their kingdom shall be re-established, and in a manner more majestic than ever before. The prophecies abound with the prom-ise of Israel's future restoration and glory, and plainly declare the day of their national repentance, and for-giveness, and of their enthronement of their Messiah at His second coming, to the throne of David, which shall be a universal throne, a world-wide kingdom of peace and righteousness which shall continue for an unbroken mil-lennium.

Back to Hosea. No sooner had the prophet uttered the prediction that Israel should "abide many days" without a kingdom, without a sacrifice, and without a priesthood, than that he declared a golden day was in store for God's nation: "AFTERWARD SHALL THE CHILDREN OF ISRAEL RETURN, AND SEEK THE LORD THEIR GOD, AND DAVID THEIR KING: and shall fear the Lord and His goodness IN THE LATTER

DAYS'' (Hos. 3:5). And to this bare all the prophets
witness. It was the song of Isaiah, the hope of Jeremiah,
the vision of Ezekiel, the dream of Daniel, and the prediction of every prophet from Moses to Malachi.

Moreover, the prophetic utterances of our Lord were
largely taken up with the glorious events pertaining to
His second coming and the restoration of the kingdom to
Israel. In His crowning discourse from the Mount of
Olives our Lord spoke plainly concerning the time of
His return and of the gathering of His people together.
Although He declared that no man could know of the
day or of the hour when He should return, it should be
remembered that He spoke definitely of the ''generation''
in which it is to occur.

The fig tree as a type of the Jewish nation is again
brought into view in the parable our Lord used in connection with the fulfillment of these prophesies: ''Now
learn a parable of the FIG TREE: when this branch
is yet tender, and putteth forth leaves, ye know that
summer is nigh; so likewise ye, WHEN YE SHALL SEE
ALL THESE THINGS, KNOW THAT IT IS NEAR,
EVEN AT THE DOORS. Verily I say unto you, THIS
GENERATION SHALL NOT PASS, TILL ALL THESE
THINGS BE FULFILLED'', (Matt. 24: 32-34).

Now, what is meant by the budding of the fig tree. It
can mean but one thing in the clear sunlight of prophecy:
THE BUDDING OF ISRAEL'S NATIONAL LIFE. That
fig tree, the nation of Israel, which was cursed by the Lord
can bear no more fruit throughout the course of this
age, but it must bear a golden harvest during the coming
age. And before a tree can bear fruit, it must first bud;
it must show signs of life. When therefore the Jews
begin to manifest signs of a revival of their national life,
then the ''summer is nigh'', the time of our Lord's glorious
return is at hand.

The question then, when were these signs to be manifested? And to this I answer that no honest student of modern history can fail to see the fulfillment of this prophecy. On December 9, 1917, General Allenby captured Jerusalem for the British, releasing the city of David from the long domination of the Turks. This significant event occurred, strangely enough, without the necessity of firing a shot. The historic Balfour declaration is well known. The Jews from over the world were permitted to return, and repossess their land. However *re-nationalization* did not occur until 1948 when the government of Israel was recognized by the United Nations.

The "fig tree" is now "budding". The greatest political miracle of all time has been witnessed in our generation. And Jesus promised that *"this generation"* (clearly, the generation which should witness the budding of the fig tree) *"shall not pass until all these things be fulfilled."* "The summer is nigh, even at the doors."

VII Destruction of the Russian Confederacy

The Destruction of the Russian Confederacy

In the light of the present world events, there is no section of the prophetic Scriptures which more intrigues me than the three chapters of Ezekiel—chapters 37, 38, and 39.

The 37th chapter has to do with the restoration of the nation of Israel to their own land of Palestine, and the following two chapters have to do with the invasion of Northern Palestine by the Northern Confederacy of Nations, headed by Russia. No events are more vividly reported than these tremendous earthshaking events.

It is our purpose to discuss this invasion of Palestine by Russia and her allies. However, as a prelude to it, we need to take a fresh look at these prophecies relating to the return of the Israelites, so that we may get a perspective of the entire picture.

God gave to Ezekiel the vision of the valley of dry bones, and the prophet saw this expansive valley of dry bones come to life again; and he was told specifically by the Lord that what he saw was prophetic of what was to happen to the house of Israel during the last days. It has to do with Israel's national resurrection. Here is a most awe-inspiring picture of the twelve tribes scattered among the nations of the earth, and being regathered, and renationalized in their own land, at the end of this age. We of this generation have lived to see the fulfillment of this prophecy.

We are, of course, well aware that Ezekiel was not the only prophet who was given to see this momentous event. Isaiah beheld these stupendous happenings as he looked through the prophetic telescope more than twenty-six hundred years ago. He reported (Isa. 11:11-12) the revelation God had given him, in these words: "And it shall come to pass in that day that the Lord shall set his hand again the second time to recover the remnant of his people, which shall be left from Assyria, and from Egypt, and (from the other nations), and from the islands of the sea. And he shall set up an ensign for the nations, and shall assemble the outcasts of Israel, and gather together the dispersed of Judah from the four corners of the earth." Others prophets—from Moses to Malachi—also made this event clear by divine revelation. But now to this amazing prophecy of Ezekiel 37: The prophet said:

"The hand of the Lord was upon me, and carried me out in the spirit of the Lord, and set me down in the midst of the valley which was full of bones, and caused me to pass by them round about: and behold, there were very many in the open valley; and, lo, they were very dry. And He said unto me, Son of man, can these bones live? And I answered, O Lord God, Thou knowest. Again He said unto me, Prophesy upon these bones, and say unto them, O ye dry bones, hear the word of the Lord. Thus saith the Lord God unto these bones: Behold, I will cause breath to enter into you, and ye shall live; and I will lay sinews upon you, and will bring flesh upon you, and cover you with skin, and put breath in you, and ye shall live: and ye shall know that I am the Lord. So I prophesied as I was commanded: and as I prophesied, there was a noise, and behold, a shaking, and the bones came together, bone to his bone. And when I beheld, lo, the sinews and flesh came upon them, and the skin covered them above: but there was no breath in them. Then said He unto me, Prophesy unto the wind, prophesy, son of man, and say to the

wind, Thus saith the Lord God: Come from the four
winds, O breath, and breathe upon these slain, that
they may live. So I prophesied as He commanded
me, and the breath came into them, and they lived,
and stood up upon their feet, an exceeding great
Army.''

And now for the interpretation of this vision-parable, read
the next four verses, (Ezekiel 37:11-14):

"Then He said unto me, Son of man, these bones
are the whole house of Israel: behold, they say, Our
bones are dried, and our hope is lost: we are cut off
for our parts. Therefore prophesy and say unto
them, Thus saith the Lord God: Behold, O My people,
I will open your graves, and cause you to come out
of your graves, and bring you into the land of Israel.
And ye shall know that I am the Lord, and when I
have opened your graves, O My people, and brought
you up out of your graves. And shall put My spirit
in you, and ye shall live, and I shall place you in your
own land: then shall ye know that I the Lord have
spoken it, and performed it, saith the Lord . . .''

Now read on, from verse 21 through verse 25:

"And say unto them, Thus saith the Lord God: Behold, I will take the children of Israel from among
the heathen, whither they be gone, and will gather
them on every side, and bring them into their own
land: and I will make them one nation in the land
upon the mountains of Israel; and one king shall
be king to them all: and they shall no more be two
nations, neither shall they be divided into two kingdoms any more at all; neither shall they defile themselves any more with their idols, nor with their de-
testable things, nor with any of their transgressions:
but I will save them out of all their dwelling places,
wherein they have sinned, and will cleanse them: so

shall they be My people, and I will be their God. **And
David My servant shall be king over them; and they
shall all have one shepherd: they shall also walk in
My judgments, and observe My statutes, to do them.**
And they shall dwell in the land that I have given
unto Jacob My servant, wherein your fathers have
dwelt; and they shall dwell therein, even they, and
their children, and their children's children for ever:
and My servant David shall be their prince forever.''

That is God's program for Israel in the last days. Already, we of this generation, have lived to see the fulfillment of much of this remarkable prophecy.

As a result of the first World War the land of Palestine was freed from the rule of the Turks. Result of the second World War was the opening of the land of Palestine for the return of the Jews, and their renationalization; and the reshuffling of the nations to prepare the way for the fulfillment of God's Word concerning the great international conflicts and the termination of the Gentile age, as set forth in the prophetic Word.

This convulsion and reshuffling of the Gentile nations is to result in the formation of two great confederacies. First, there must be the completion of the Northern Confederation, headed up by Soviet Russia, and which shall include all her satellite nations, plus some of the great Asiatic powers. Then, there is to be the Western confederation of nations, which will include the nations comprising all the territory of the ancient Roman Empire. The final form of this latter confederacy, as we noted, is to be a ten-power kingdom.

As is well known, both the Northern and the Western confederacies are in the process of formation, and except for a few development, are well-nigh completed. And so the stage is being set for the enactment of the world's final drama. And what a drama it shall be!

This much I have said in order to introduce you to the amazing prophecies of these two great chapters—Chapters 38 and 39 of Ezekiel. At the beginning of Chapter 38, we have a picture of the Northern Confederacy marching down on Palestine. Read the first four verses:

> "And the word of the Lord came unto me, saying, Son of man, set they face against Gog, the land of Magog, the chief prince of Meshech and Tubal, and prophesy against him, and say, Thus saith the Lord God, Behold, I am against thee, O Gog, the chief prince of Meshech and Tubal: and I will turn thee back, and put hooks into thy jaws, and I will bring thee forth, and all thine army, horses and horsemen, all of them clothed with all sorts of armour, even a great company with bucklers and shields, all of them handling swords."

In these first six verses we have the clear identification of Russia as the fountain-head of this Northern Confederation. The land of Magog has long been identified as Russia by the historians. The name "Gog" is the prince of the land, Magog. He is also called the prince of Meschech and Tubal, meaning, of course, Russia's principal cities of Moscow and Tobolsk.

This passage also reveals the names of the nations which are associated with Russia in this confederacy. Some of these names are slightly different from the names of those nations today, for we must bear in mind that this prophecy was given some twenty-five centuries ago, and the prophecy was undoubtedly penned in the language which was understood by those who should read it in Ezekiel's day. However, in the light of history, those nations are identifiable. Now, these nations, headed by Communistic Russia shall march at God's appointed time, and not one hour sooner, south to Palestine.

The reason given for their march south into Palestine is to take a spoil. Mark the words in verse 11 and 12 where the specific purpose is stated: "I will go up to the land of unwalled villages . . . to take a spoil, and to take a prey, to turn thine hand upon the desolate places that are now inhabited, and upon the people that are gathered out of the nations."

Today Russia covets the rich oil fields of Iran: approximately one thousand wells in the Middle East. Only the fear of annihilation by atomic warfare has hindered her from occupying those countries to the north of Palestine. But when the hour-hand of God's prophetic time clock strikes twelve, Russia will take the risk.

Included in the coveted spoils is the immense wealth of the Dead Sea. This Sea is 1292 feet below sea level, and at its northern end is thirteen hundred feet deep. Its fabulous mineral deposits astound the imagination. It has been found that from two hundred feet down there is a heavy solution of minerals of great value, both to modern industry and war. Such minerals as potassium, chloride, magnesium, sodium chloride, and many others are found in abundance. A British corporation known as Potash Limited explored the wealth of this fabulous Sea, and now huge operations are underway on the shores of these historic waters, located only 22 miles from Jerusalem.

Russia will go down there "to take a spoil". And there is every reason to believe that Russia is ambitious to eventually capture and control the Suez Canal. If they could control the Suez Canal, they could accomplish the economic strangulation of Western Europe. So, there are a number of reasons why Russia would like to expand southward.

Now, the prophet Ezekiel pictures this huge combination of nations moving into Northern Palestine. "They shall come against My people Israel as a cloud to cover the land.'' This suggests an aerial invasion. Russia has enough aircraft today to literally cover as a cloud the land of Palestine. It is also significant that cavalry will play a large role in this invasion. They shall come ''riding upon horses, a great company, and a mighty army''. Today Russia has about 70 per cent of the world's horses, and the finest breeding stock. Crossbred with the Arabian horse, the Russian horse today is the most fleetfooted of any cavalry units anywhere in the world.

But this dreaded Northern Confederation of Nations shall be stopped suddenly, right in their tracks, in northern Palestine, and the most complete destruction of those armies shall be accomplished by the judgment of Almighty God, perhaps through a mighty earthquake. Five out of every six troops shall be destroyed.

From Chapter 39 (vss. 1-12) we read:

> ''Therefore, thou son of man, prophesy against Gog and say, Thus saith the Lord God: Behold, I am against thee, O Gog, the chief prince of Meschech and Tubal; and I will turn thee back, and leave but the sixth part of thee, and will cause thee to come up from the north parts, and will bring thee upon the mountains of Israel: and I will smite thy bow out of thy left hand, and will cause thine arrows to fall out of thy right hand. Thou shalt fall upon the mountains of Israel, thou, and all thy bands, and the people that is with thee: I will give thee unto the ravenous birds of every sort, and to the beasts of the field to be devoured. Thou shalt fall upon the open field: for I have spoken it, saith the Lord God. And I will send a fire on Magog, and among them that dwell carelessly in the isles: and they shall know that I am the Lord. So will I make My holy Name known in the midst of My people Israel; and I will not let them pollute My holy Name any more: and the heathen shall know

that I am the Lord, the Holy One in Israel. Behold, it is come, and it is done, saith the Lord God; this is the day whereof I have spoken. And they that dwell in the cities of Israel shall go forth, and shall set on fire and burn the weapons, both the shields and the bucklers, the bows and the arrows, and the handstaves, and the spears, and they shall burn them with fire seven years: so that they shall take no wood out of the field, neither cut down any out of the forests; for they shall burn the weapons with fire: and they shall spoil those that spoiled them, and rob those that robbed them, saith the Lord God. And it shall come to pass in that day, that I will give unto Gog a place there of graves in Israel, the valley of the passengers on the east of the sea: and it shall stop the noses of the passengers: and there shall they bury Gog and all his multitude: and they shall call it the valley of Hamon-gog And seven months shall the house of Israel be burying them, that they may cleanse the land.''

When shall these tremendous events occur? God said, through the prophet Ezekiel, that it would be ''in the latter years'', verse 8: and ''in the latter days'', verse 16. And quite specifically it does not happen until Israel is back in her land, dwelling safely, or confidently. Today Israel is confident of her security. She feels that if trouble comes abundant help will come from her allies. But Israel, in her present apostate condition, is not depending upon the true and living God and the Father of our Lord Jesus Christ for deliverance. She is yet in the darkness of unbelief, as yet unwilling to recognize in Jesus of Nazareth the Messiah who came to redeem her. But what a wonderful day that will be when the scales shall fall from the people's eyes, and they shall acknowledge

Christ as the Son of God, as their Messiah, and as the One who shall sit upon David's throne.

Friends, when these terrible events mentioned in Ezekiel 37 and 38 are taking place, the church will not be here to witness it, for every born-again soul will be caught up to be with the Lord in the glorious rapture.

I emphasize that we are in the closing days of this age. What we do for Christ, we must do now, for soon we shall hear the call, "Behold, the Bridegroom cometh; go ye out to meet Him". Let us be sure that our lamps are trimmed and burning bright.

We are still in the day of grace for the unbelieving world. If some of you are without the assurance of eternal life, if you have not trusted in the Lord Jesus Christ as your Saviour, then I remind you that God loves you, and it was for you that Christ died. He will yet receive you, even today, if you will put your faith and trust in Him. As God's messenger, I invite you to receive Him now, and know the joy of sins forgiven. "Whosoever shall call upon the Name of the Lord shall be saved," (Rom. 10:13).

VIII The Last World Government

The Last World Government

In a previous discussion, we pointed out that immediately prior to the establishing of the Millennial Kingdom of Christ on the earth, there will be a powerful government, the ultimate in human government, and containing all the elements of decay and degradation. The Stone "cut out without hands", which the prophet Daniel saw, fell on the toes of this mighty colossus, and broke it to pieces, and it became like the chaff of the summer threshing floors.

This powerful earthly government will not be one single nation, but a community of nations, a federation of ten nations. The number of nations in this confederation is mentioned in three different prophecies: First, the ten toes of Nebuchadnezzar's image; second, the ten horns of the beast of Daniel 7, which is a parallel prophecy to that of Daniel 2; and third, in the description of the Beast of Revelation 13, a mighty earth ruler, the Man of Sin, which is pictured with ten horns.

This ten-power kingdom is to be a revival of the ancient Roman Empire, and is to include the same territory of the Caesars, with additional territories. We know precisely what that territory included, and we know what it did not include. We know that it did not include Russia, nor any of the nations associated with her, presently known as satellites. Certain nations which are at present under Soviet domination will undergo a change, and will swing back into the Western orbit. This northern confederacy is something different from the revived Roman empire, and completely antagonistic to it.

We are concerned at present with the nature of this Western confederacy. Forerunner of this ten-power kingdom is, we believe, NATO (North Atlantic Treaty Organization). In its final form it will not include all the nations it now embraces. It will become solidified, and take on a rigid form. But it will contain the seeds of its own destruction; for, as Daniel saw the ten toes of the image were as mixed clay and iron, it is to be a kingdom representing various types of government, and varying forms of philosophy. A very powerful ruler will forge these component parts together into what will appear to be an invincible world power. But when we examine the nature of this ten-power kingdom, we see that it is completely corrupt.

It is quite clear that it is materialistic in outlook. There will be a greater dependence upon physical reserves, and natural resources, and war machinery. There is nothing, utterly nothing in this last great world empire which is spiritual, nothing which honors the God of heaven.

Its culture is humanistic. Everywhere the ingenuity of man will be emphasized. All credit for all progress will be ascribed to mankind. There will be a worship of the creature rather than the Creator. Shrines will be erected to the gods of science, industry, commerce and war. Man's accomplishments shall be the inspiration for worship. And this philosophy of humanism will ultimately find expression in the worship of a man, who will be worshipped as God.

We see, further, that in the nature of this final earthly kingdom, there will be the spirit of atheism. It will be an anti-God movement. Humanism rules God out. As this spirit of man-worship grows, antagonism against God will be more and more manifest, until, finally, humanity, as expressed through this last world government, will be in war against God Almighty.

Parallel with the development of materialism, humanism, and atheism will be the collectivism which will completely destroy individualism, or private enterprise. Huge combines in the world of industry, commerce, banking and agriculture, will deliver the control of mankind, first, to a few powerful individuals, and finally to the control of one man. Liberty will glimmer, fade, and vanish from the earth. Education will be completely standardized, and thoroughly sovietized. Everybody will be required to think after a certain set pattern.

Religion, also, will be unified. There will be one giant ecclesiastical octopus. All religion will be made to fit into the pattern of this godless materialistic philosophy of Antichrist. If any are unwilling, they shall be compelled to follow the pattern of Antichrist. "And he causeth all, both small and great, rich and poor, free and bond, to receive a mark in their right hand, or in their foreheads: and that no man might buy or sell, save he that had the mark, or the name of the beast, or the number of his name," (Rev. 13:16, 17). True spiritual worship of God, the God of Heaven, and of Jesus Christ, His Son, will not be allowed.

Such is the prophetic picture of that last world government of men, in its final horrible form. A dismal, gloomy, fearful picture, but an accurate picture of man's attempt to rule without God. Already, in every department of human life, we see the lengthening shadows of these godless trends. Already, the culture of our modern society is rotting at the core. Godless materialism marches on. The sinister clouds of atheism are lowering over the horizon.

To bring to full fruition the awful scope and sway of this last world kingdom, there must be a leader, the world's most unusual leader, a veritable superman. The character, nature and the power of this man are described in many prophetic Scriptures. He is called by different names, such as: The Man of Sin, the Beast, the Antichrist.

He shall be the incarnation of Satan, in the same way that Christ was the incarnation of God. All the hellish qualities of Satan shall indwell this man of sin; the spirit of the pit shall control him utterly. He shall receive his power from the devil—as we read in Revelation 13:2: "And the dragon gave him his power, and his seat, and great authority." As Daniel said: "His power shall be mighty, but not by his own power." Quite literally, his reign shall be the reign of hell on earth.

Some of his characteristics should be noted. We are told that through craft, and deceit, and through counterfeit peace offers he shall destroy many, (Dan. 8). Although described as a man of "fierce countenance", he will doubtless have a magnetic personality, and many will follow him instantly, and will become so completely loyal to him that they will gladly die as pawns in his hands. All the power of Satanic subtlety will be his. He will be the world's most clever diplomat. Diplomacy is the big word in international relations today. (The word, we know, is a derivative of the same word from which we get the word "duplicity", actually meaning "deception"). Antichrist will be the greatest deceiver the world has ever known.

But he shall be characterized, also, by self-exaltation. Daniel said, "He shall magnify himself in his heart," (Dan. 8:25). Paul reminded the Thessalonians that Christ's personal return would not occur until . . . "that man of sin be revealed, the son of perdition, who opposeth and exalteth himself above all that is called God, or that is worshipped, so that he as God sitteth in the temple of God, showing himself that he is God," (2 Thess. 2:3, 4). He is to be the greatest boaster, the greatest braggart, the greatest presumer ever to appear on the horizon of human history.

Other prophetic Scriptures describes this coming super-man as cruel, fierce, inhuman, **bloodthirsty**—a dictator completely without conscience. So terrible will be his reign that it is described as the Great Tribulation. His all-consuming ambition shall be to rule the world, destroy the righteous, and be worshipped as God.

And this leads us to the final description concerning this Man of Sin. He shall blaspheme the name of the Lord, and war against God. Daniel said, "He shall stand up against the Prince of princes," (Dan. 8:25). Paul prophesied that this godless presumer would sit in the temple, and declare that he was God; that he would "oppose" God, and exalt himself above all that is called God," (2 Thess. 2:4); and concerning him in Revelation 13, we read that "he opened his mouth in blasphemy against God, to blaspheme His name, and His tabernacle, and them that dwell in heaven," (Rev. 13:6).

Our Lord recalled the prophecy of Daniel concerning the Satanic activities of Antichrist, and said, "When ye therefore shall see the abomination of desolation, spoken of by Daniel the prophet, stand in the holy place, then let them which be in Judea flee into the mountains . . . for then shall be great tribulation such as was not since the beginning of the world to this time, no, nor ever shall be."

And all this is tied in with the personal, visible return of Christ, for He said: "Immediately after the tribulation of those days shall the sun be darkened, and the moon shall not give her light, and the stars shall fall from heaven, and the powers of the heavens shall be shaken: and then shall appear the sign of the Son of man in heaven: and then shall all the tribes of the earth mourn, and they shall see the Son of man coming in the clouds of heaven, with power and great glory. And He shall send His angels with a great sound of a trumpet, and they shall gather together His elect from the four winds, from one end of heaven to the other," (Matt. 24:29-31).

Then comes the doom of the Antichrist and his false prophet, and all the enemies of the Lord. As we read in Second Thessalonians, 1:7-10: "And to you who are troubled, rest with us, when the Lord Jesus Christ shall be revealed from heaven with His mighty angels, in flaming fire, taking vengeance on them that know not God, and that obey not the Gospel of our Lord Jesus Christ: who shall be punished with everlasting destruction from the presence of the Lord, and from the glory of His power; when He shall come to be glorified in His saints, and to be admired in all them that believe . . . in that day.'' And Chapter 2, verse 8: ''And then shall that Wicked be revealed, whom the Lord shall consume with the spirit of His mouth, and shall destroy with the brightness of His coming.''

''And I saw heaven opened, and behold a white horse; and He that sat upon him was called Faithful and True, and in righteousness He doth judge and make war. His eyes were as a flame of fire, and on His head were many crowns, and He had a name written, that no man knew, but He Himself. And He was clothed with a vesture dipped in blood: and His name is called The Word of God. And the armies which were in heaven followed Him upon white horses, clothed in fine linen, white and clean. And out of His mouth goeth a sharp sword, that with it He should smite the nations: and He shall rule them with a rod of iron: and He treadeth the winepress of the fierceness and wrath of Almighty God. And He hath on His vesture and on His thigh a name written, KING OF KINGS, AND LORD OF LORDS. . . . And the beast was taken, and with him the false prophet that wrought miracles before him, with which he deceived them that had received the mark of the beast, and them that worshipped his image. These both were cast alive into a lake of fire burning with brimstone,'' (Rev. 19:11-16, 20).

IX The Kingdom of God

The Kingdom Of God

The Bible teaches that God rules, and rules with absolute authority over the entire realm of His creation. This is also a self-evident truth. The God who had the power, and the wisdom, and the might to create a universe like this, and to create the Universe of universes, must of necessity be a God who is able to sustain, and to maintain the minute mechanism of all His marvelous creation.

If He were to cease to be the kind of a God He is just for one minute, or if He were to divorce Himself from His creation, and divest Himself of His absolute sovereignty, every star and planet in the stellar heavens would melt in a sea of fervent heat, disintegrate into gases, and every created thing, both animate and inanimate would cease to be forever.

Let us, first, consider the nature of God's kingdom, as revealed in the Scriptures:

It is *universal*. I Chron. 29:11-12; states: "Thine, O Lord, is the greatness, and the power, and the glory, and the victory, and the majesty: for all that is in the heaven and in the earth is Thine; Thine is the kingdom, O Lord, and Thou art exalted as head above all." Again, Psalm 103:19: "The Lord hath prepared His throne in the heavens; and His kingdom ruleth over all."

It is *timeless* in character. His kingdom is eternal. Lam. 5:19: "Thou, O Lord, remainest forever; Thy throne from generation to generation." Ps. 10:16: "The Lord is King for ever and ever." Jer. 10:10: "But the Lord is the true God, He is the living God, and an everlasting king." It is clear from these and many other Scriptures that God has always possessed absolute sovereignty, and reigns as king.

It is a kingdom of *righteousness and truth.* As the God of all holiness and righteousness, and truth, and infinite justice, He is the moral Governor of the Universe which He has made, and the end of all things is for His glory. The purpose of every created being, from the tiniest form of life up to angels and archangels, is for God's glory. This is true with regard to God's special and most favored creation—man. The Lord has created man for His glory.

God's government on this earth is through men by divine appointment. Dan. 4:17: "The most High ruleth in the kingdom of men, and giveth it to whomsoever He will." Again, in verse 25, we note that God told king Nebuchadnezzar that he would be driven from his seat of power, as head of the Babylonian empire, to dwell with the beasts of the field—how long? Listen to the Word of God: "Till thou know that the most High ruleth in the kingdom of men, and giveth it to whomsoever He will." Proverbs 21:1 declares that "The king's heart is in the hand of the Lord." This means that God directs the conduct of kings to fulfill His purpose.

Many rulers have not acknowledged the sovereignty of God; many have not recognized this fact, but have rather despised God's commandments—nevertheless God has used them to fulfill His purposes in government. To some wicked rulers, such as king Pharaoh, God hardened their hearts in order to fulfill His purposes. Let us remember that no ruler can exercise authority over men without God's appointment. Men become heads of states and countries through either the directive or the permissive will of God.

Thus we are enjoined by Paul in the 13th chapter of Romans, to submit to earthly authority: "Let every soul be subject unto the higher powers. For there is no power but of God: *the powers that be are ordained of God.* Whosoever therefore resisteth the power (that is, the government) resisteth the ordinance of God: and they that resist shall receive to themselves damnation.'' Then, speaking of the earthly governor or ruler, Paul said, "He is the minister of God,'' the servant of God. And, we know that our Lord respected earthly government, for He commanded to "Render unto Caesar the things which are Caesar's, and unto God the things which are God's.''

Earthly rulers, then, are appointed of God, and are called the servants of God in fulfilling His purpose in earthly government. They are rulers, but they are not sovereign rulers, for God Almighty, the Most High God of heaven and earth has never surrendered His sovereignty to any man; nor has he ever shared it with men. It is well that we fix this important fact in our minds. Otherwise, it would be difficult for us to understand the nature of God's government among men.

Now, we have seen that the nature of God's kingdom is that it is universal; it is timeless in character, for it is an eternal kingdom; it is a kingdom of righteousness and truth. And we have seen that God's government on this earth is through men by His divine appointment. This leads us, now, to consider the plan God has revealed for His "theocracy.'' This is the name of God's program of government on this earth.

For thousands of years we have classified earthly governments as Monarchies, or as Autocracies, or in more recent times, as Democracies. But none of these is God's ideal form of Government. God's plan is the Theocracy, which means that the Lord Himself is the true ruler, and that He rules through the appointment of men. This perfect system of government can only come, and will surely come when the rulers appointed, and all the people, have in their hearts the love of God, and desire only to fulfill His will.

As yet, we have never seen such a system as this, but it shall come in all its glorious reality when the Millennial kingdom is established. Christ shall establish this kingdom, and His sovereignty shall be exercised, and it shall be recognized and acknowledged by all. Such will be a kingdom of peace and righteousness. Now, the establishment of such a kingdom by our Lord is not an afterthought, but rather a program which was set forth immediately after the creation of man. For it was at that time that God gave man the commandment to subdue the earth and have dominion over it, (Gen. 1:28).

God's perfect kingdom on this earth would have been a natural development if Adam had been true to his trust. This Theocracy would have become a glorious reality. But Adam failed God, as did Eve, in the temptation, and rebelled against the revealed will of God. It was at this stage that Satan began to presume a place of authority over men. And it was then that the Lord God pronounced a curse upon man, and even upon the earth itself.

However, let us keep this important fact well in our minds: God never abandoned His plan to rule through men on this earth. His program of redemption was immediately set forth, and He promised that "the Seed of Woman shall bruise the serpent's head." It was through the line of Seth that God began to establish government on the earth.

But the wickedness of men became so great that God sent the flood to destroy all flesh, save Noah and his family who found grace in the eyes of the Lord. And after the flood God spoke directly of the formation of human government. The terms of such government were outlined in the covenant with Noah, as given in the 9th chapter of Genesis.

Again, this stage of the program was interrupted by gross corruption, and it was Nimrod who set it aside, and established something of his own choosing, as he was under the dominion of Satan. He even set up a new religion. Now, at this stage, God called Abraham, and established through him the Theocracy, which was patriarchal in character. The patriarchs of those generations—Abraham, Isaac, Jacob, and the children of Israel.

This form of government—or, we should say this form of God's Theocracy, continued on for many generations, until it reached its highest form during the period of the Judges. These Judges were appointed of God, and ruled the nation of Israel. However, even under such ideal conditions, the children of Israel became disobedient, times without number, and were again, and again taken captive by other nations, only, in turn, to be delivered by the providence and power of God. Finally, they even rebelled against that form of the Theocracy, and demanded that they should do away with that system, and be as the other nations, and establish a national kingdom, and have a king. But the king they selected—King Saul—proved to be a total failure. At this stage, God ordained the prophet Samuel to annoint David as king.

God's plan for the Theocracy was still in the process. And the Lord entered into a covenant with David that this kingdom would become that government of God in the earth, and that David's Seed, (not seeds, as of many, but Seed, as one) even Christ, as David's son would sit upon the throne of this Theocracy, and would fulfill God's purpose in executing and administering righteous government in the earth.

It was concerning this glorious kingdom that the prophets sang, and for centuries which followed brought hope to the nation of Israel, and of Judah, even while they were in captivity, and scattered among the nations. Now, it is this Theocracy, this political form of government which will be the establishment of the Kingdom of God on earth. It will be called the kingdom of Christ because He shall reign, in Person, from Jerusalem, and through His appointed governors and servants.

And it is crystal-clear that no such kingdom has ever yet prevailed on this earth, unless indeed it was established at the Garden of Eden. I emphasize this fact because nowadays you hear a great deal about "establishing the kingdom of God on earth" through the work of the church.

But nowhere in the Word of God will you ever find the remotest suggestion that it is the purpose of the church to establish God's temporal kingdom, or the kingdom of Christ, on this earth. The church occupies a different sphere in God's program. There is certainly the revelation that we enter "the kingdom of heaven" through Christ, and in the broad sense of the word, we are a part of God's spiritual kingdom. But the kingdom of Christ, as a temporal, earthly kingdom will not, and cannot be established until Christ returns.

We believe the time of this glorious day of God's rule of this earth is fast approaching. However, in the clear sunlight of prophecy, before this great event occurs, the church, that is, all born again believers will be caught up in the rapture, at the sound of the trumpet; and, afterwards, for a few brief years the dreadful kingdom of the antichrist, and the judgments which shall fall. Then the personal appearance of Christ on the Mount of Olives, when every eye shall see Him . . . and He shall judge the nations, and forthwith establish His kingdom, and reign for a thousand years. This will be the kingdom of God on earth.

X Christ's Millennial Kingdom

Christ's Millennial Kingdom

A golden age is approaching, a time for this earth when all the hopes and aspirations of men shall be fulfilled. Catching the strain of the prophets of Zion, the whole world has joined in the song of that blessed age to come —the glorious millennial kingdom. However, those who have departed from the prophetic Scriptures have formed many different opinions as to what the Millennium will be like.

As to how the Millennium shall be ushered in, there are as many opinions as there are schools of political philosophy. We shall not waste our time in exploring the vagaries of human speculations. Just as "men by wisdom know not God," so also men are ignorant concerning a system of world government which will assure peace and tranquility, and plenty, for all mankind.

The one form of government that will bring about ideal political, social, and moral conditions is a Theocracy—a government in which God Himself shall rule. Countless other systems have been tried. All have failed. But the millennial kingdom will be such a theocracy. It shall be established by the Son of God, in person, when He returns in power and glory.

To establish such a kingdom every vestige of human government must first be abolished, and what is more, Satan must be completely subdued, and put out of the way. How this is to be accomplished is dramatically described in Revelation 20:1-3:

> "And I saw an angel come down from heaven, having the key to the bottomless pit and a great chain in

his hand. And he laid hold on the dragon, that old serpent, which is the Devil, and Satan, and bound him a thousand years. And cast him into the bottomless pit, and shut him up, and set a seal upon him, that he should deceive the nations no more, till the thousand years should be fulfilled.''

And, of course, there can be no Millennium without a millennial King. Jesus Christ shall be that King, and His saints shall reign with Him. ''And I saw thrones, and they sat upon them, and judgment was given unto them.'' Concerning such a kingdom all the prophets bear witness.

Isaiah, preeminently the kingdom prophet, foresaw the time when Israel should be re-gathered in their own land, with Messiah as their King, and as the king of the whole world, reigning in peace and righteousness:

''And the government shall be upon His shoulder: and His name shall be called Wonderful, Counsellor, The mighty God, The Everlasting Father, the Prince of Peace. Of the increase of His government and peace there shall be no end'' (Isa. 9:6-7).

''And it shall come to pass in that day, that the Lord shall set His hand again the second time to recover the remnant of His people . . . And He shall set up an ensign for the nations, and shall assemble the outcasts of Israel, and gather together the dispersed of Judah from the four corners of the earth,'' (Isa. 11:11, 12).

Think of what it will mean to have a cessation of wars, and even the threat of wars, where perfect peace shall reign for an entire millennium; a kingdom ruled by the love of God; and one in which the King shall have a personal and benevolent interest in every subject!

In addition to a righteous government, politically perfect, there shall be many wonderful changes wrought in the earth. It is prophecied that immediately before the coming of the King there shall be earthquakes of immense proportions, also a shaking up of the heavenlies. The physiognomy of the earth will doubtless be changed in many areas. Atmospheric conditions will be greatly improved, so that the seasons of the earth will be perfect everywhere. Climate throughout the inhabited world will be ideal.

All through this age, since the fall of Adam, there has been a curse resting upon the physical earth, (Gen. 3:17). Every time we see a thorn or thistle it is a silent reminder of this fact. The whole of the earthly creation is sighing for that day when it shall be delivered from the bondage and curse resting upon it, (Rom. 8:22-24). In that day "the wilderness and the solitary place shall be glad, and the desert shall rejoice and blossom as the rose. It shall rejoice abundantly . . . for in the wilderness shall water break out, and streams in the desert. And the parched ground shall become a pool, and the thirsty land springs of water," Isa. 35:1, 2, 6.

There shall also be a marvelous change wrought in the animal kingdom. The enmity between mankind and animals since the time of the Edenic curse shall be removed. There was a day when man had the dominion over the whole creation, (Gen. 1:28), but man's disobedience brought about an awful change. But we look for that glorious restoration as described in Isa. 11:6-9: "The wolf shall dwell with the lamb, and the leopard shall lie down with the kid; and the calf and the young lion and the fatling together; a little child shall lead them . . . and the suckling child shall play on the hole of the asp, and the weaned child shall put his hands on the cockatrice den. They shall not hurt nor destroy."

Moreover, the blessings that shall come to the physical life of mankind shall be no less wonderful. During the Millennium, "The inhabitants shall not say, I am sick,"

(Isa. 33:24). All physical defects and imperfections shall be remedied: "In that day shall the deaf hear the words of the book and the eyes of the blind shall see out of obscurity and out of darkness." (Isa. 29:18). Also, "The heart of the rash shall understand knowledge,. and the tongue of the stammerers shall be made to speak plainly." (Isa. 32:4).

Conditions of life for all the lowly will be greatly blessed: "The meek also shall increase their joy in the Lord, and the poor among men shall rejoice in the Holy One of Israel," (Isa. 29:19). All these circumstances shall be conducive to long life, for we read again in Isa. 65:20-23 that "there shall be no more infant of days, nor an old man that hath not filled his days; for the child shall die an hundred years old; but the sinner being an hundred years old shall be accursed. And they shall build houses, and inhabit them; and they shall plant vineyards and eat the fruit of them. They shall not build and another inhabit; they shall not plant, and another eat; for as the days of a tree are the days of my people, and mine elect shall long enjoy the work of their hands. They shall not labour in vain, nor bring forth for trouble; for they are the seed of the blessed of the LORD and their offspring with them."

Now, in addition, one of the most glowing of all considerations concerning this Millennial Age is the moral transformation of the inhabitants of the earth. Satan being bound and cast into the abyss, sin will be practically abolished. The only kind of sin possible will be in the nature of individual and willful rebellion against the King of the earth, and Scripture warrants the assumption that this will be very exceptional and rare, and such as are guilty will immediately "perish from the way," (Ps. 2:12). For when righteousness "reigns" it must have universal sway. There can be no deception on the earth because the arch deceiver is out of the way during this reign.

Jeremiah tells us that God has promised a new covenant for that era: "I will put My law in their inward parts, and write it in their hearts; and will be their God, and they shall be my people. And they shall teach no more every man his neighbor, and every man his brother saying, Know the Lord; for they shall all know Me, from the least of them unto the greatest of them, saith the Lord." (Jer. 31:33-34). And the prophet Joel adds that, "In that day I will pour out my spirit upon all flesh, saith the Lord."

From these Scriptures, and many others that might be cited, it is clear that there will be a change in the moral fabric of human society such as no reform movement could ever hope to bring about; for the world at heart shall be transformed. They shall come to recognize the mighty One of Israel as not only the great and only perfect King in the temporal realm, but also as "The Holy One," the one and only King in the spiritual realm, and will enthrone Him in their own hearts, and give to Him the worship and the honor and the glory of which He has been so truly deserving since the world began.

Pre-eminently, the Kingdom Age shall be one of Righteousness and Peace. There can never be a universal reign of righteousness on this earth until He comes "Whose name is called Faithful and True, and in righteousness doth He judge and make war" (Rev. 19:11-16). To "judge and make war" on the Beast and the host of rebels gathered against Him at His coming. But the triumph shall come in lightning swiftness. Then, no more war! All nations shall then disarm: "And they shall beat their swords into plowshares, and their spears into pruning hooks: nation shall not lift up sword against nation, neither shall they learn war any more," Isa. 2:2-4.

When all implements of war are converted into implements of peace, the world will no longer have need of international arbitration councils, or peace conferences. No more unrest for this world when the Prince of Peace sits upon His throne!

XI When Will Christ Return? (Pre-Post- or A-Millennial)

When Will Christ Return?

(Pre- Post- or A- Millennial)

The question as to when Christ shall return is of primary importance. It is not necessary that we should know of the exact date. Concerning this supreme event Jesus said, "Of that day and hour knoweth no man, no, not even the angels of heaven, but My Father only," Matt. 24:36.

And, in His last words with His disciples, our Lord emphasized, "It is not for you to know the times and the seasons which the Father hath put in His own power," Acts 1:7.

But, although we cannot know of the exact date, we most assuredly can know the approximate date of His coming. There are many prophecies which speak of events which are to occur immediately prior to our Lord's return. There are equally as many other prophecies which cannot be fulfilled until He returns, and afterward.

Nevertheless, around these predictions a controversy has raged for many generations. Two schools of thought set forth quite distinctly different views. The "premillennialists" believe Christ is coming before the Millennium, or to establish His kingdom on earth and reign for one thousand years. The theory of the "postmillennialists" is that Christ will not return until after the thousand years have been fulfilled.

Still a third theory has developed within the past generation, which is neither "pre-" nor "post-." It is called "amillennialism". This fantastic interpretation of Biblical eschatology was developed by a few disillusioned postmillennialists. Their fanciful opinions, based on purely figurative interpretations, are as illogical as they are un-Scriptural. But we shall return to the amillennialist heresy after we have examined the postmillennial theory in contrast to the premillennial position.

In a previous discussion we have pointed out the fact that the entertainment of the "blessed hope" of our Lord's return affects the life, the walk, and the conversation of the believer. But it is obvious that if the postmillennial theory were true, and we could not expect the return of Christ for another thousand years, then the hope loses its power in the life of the Christian. For, if the program of the church is to gradually Christianize the social order, as the postmillennialists teach, then the outlook today, in the light of present world conditions, could only be discouraging and despairing. With the small measure of success by the church to "build the kingdom of God on earth", it would seem that we may have to wait for at least a million years to realize such an unscriptural goal.

Now, before examining the true nature of the heresy of postmillennialism, it will be well that we trace in history the development of the spirit of unbelief in the literal fulfillment of prophecy.

During the early centuries of the Christian era, the literal character of the Bible prophecies was unchallenged by the churches. Writings of the Christian leaders reveal clearly that they believed in the literal fulfillment of all the prophecies pertaining to the personal return of Christ to establish His kingdom on the earth and reign for a thousand years. They simply assumed these inspired teachings to be true, exactly as they assumed and accepted the doctrines of the Deity of Christ, His vicarious death, His resurrection from the dead, His ascension, and His present priesthood in heaven. They all looked forward to the time when their Lord should come again to destroy the works of the devil, bind Satan, and establish a kingdom of righteousness.

However, when the church of Rome became so powerful during the fourth century, and later, the teaching was projected that Christ's kingdom was now being established, and that when the Church of Rome conquered the world, the kingdom promised by the Lord Jesus Christ would become a reality; and so they were to strive for that goal.

It is true that the Church of Rome held sway for a thousand years; but instead of being a kingdom of light, it was a kingdom of darkness; instead of being a kingdom of righteousness, it became a kingdom of spiritual wickedness. The Roman church tried to remove the Book of Revelation from the sacred canon, because certain portions of this book prophecy concerning the destruction of a certain corrupt ecclesiastical organization (chapters 17-18); they wanted to discount the last book of the Bible, but they were unable to prove that it was not inspired. So what they did was to prohibit the people from reading the Bible. They hid the Bible, and it therefore became a closed book for over one thousand years. Except for some small sects of Christians, such as the Anabaptists and the Waldenses who managed to preserve the Scriptures in spite of Rome, the Bible was hidden.

At length, after the Protestant Reformation, the Scriptures began to be published again, and with the invention of printing, thousands of copies of God's Book were circulated. Once more, the study of prophecy was revived, and all Bible-believers accepted the literalness of all the prophetic Scriptures. However, certain state churches which developed began to discourage belief in the literal fulfillment of prophecies concerning the return of the Jews to Palestine, the reign of Antichrist, the Great Tribulation, the Battle of Armageddon, and the personal return of Christ. They made exactly the same error that was made by the Church of Rome—they taught that *their* powerful state church, coming out of the Roman church, was the beginning of the Millennium. The prophetic Scrip-

tures became obnoxious to the leaders of the state churches
because those Scriptures reveal that the ecclesiastical au-
thorities will fail in their effort to bring in the kingdom,
and that many of the church leaders will prove to be false
guides, and will receive a severe condemnation when Christ
comes.

So the problem of these religious leaders was to discredit prophecy in the minds of the common people. It
was a very great obstacle. How could they discredit
prophecy and at the same time expect the people to believe
that the Bible was inspired?

A certain English churchman named Daniel Whitby,
in the early 18th century, worked out what seemed to be
a solution to the problem. He called his idea the "new
hypothesis." It was certainly well named. It was an
hypothesis, which means an "unproven theory" or a
guess. It was certainly new, because it was not taught in
the Bible. It was the theory of postmillennialism. He
classed most of the prophecies as "figurative". Every
prophecy which seemed to teach the imminent return of
Christ was put into that category. His theory did not
deny that Christ would return, but rather that He would
not come until after the thousand years of peace and righteousness on the earth; that the church would set up the
kingdom of God on the earth. This was the beginning
of postmillennialism. The idea soon had wide acceptance
on the part of churchmen, and was taught in the seminaries. Thus developed the program of "Christianizing
society". The mission of the church was declared to be
to "make the world a better place in which to live." As a
result of this teaching whole denominations began to lose
sight of the Great Commission to evangelize the world by
the preaching of the crucified and risen Saviour. They
lost sight of the fact that Christ was to return to rapture
the church, to judge the nations, and to establish His
own kingdom of peace and righteousness.

Thus we see how the ancient error of the Church of Rome, and the later Protestant state church error, was now reintroduced and promoted by postmillennialism.

However, God has seen fit to maintain for Himself a witness through all these generations. There have been those minorities within the ecclesiastical bodies who have kept the flame of premillennial truth burning. They have not conformed to the unscriptural traditions of man-made creeds, but have steadfastly contended for a literal interpretation of these wonderful Bible prophecies.

When it is made crystal-clear in the 20th chapter of Revelation that Christ's coming is to be before the millennium, then it is important that we believe this plain and simple teaching. This, then, is the difference between the "pre" and the "post" millennial positions. Premillenarians believe in the literal fulfillment of prophecy; and postmillennialists deny the literal fulfillment of God's inspired Word.

Never has there been a theory of Bible interpretation offered which has such a lame foundation, from a purely Scriptural standpoint, as that of postmillennialism. There is not one single statement in the Word of God that teaches, either directly or indirectly, or inferentially, that Christ is not to return until after a thousand years of peace and righteousness on the earth. The only hope of the postmillennialists in the support of their theory is to *spiritualize* certain Scriptures, wresting them from their true meaning, and framing them to fit into their idealistic philosophy. As an illustration of this they take the parable of the leaven which our Lord gave:

"The kingdom of heaven is like unto leaven, which a woman took, and hid in three measures of meal, till the whole was leavened," (Matt. 13:33).

They teach from this that leaven is truth and righteousness, but Jesus makes it clear that leaven is "evil doctrine".

In order to support their theory, they deliberately ignore literally scores of plain Scripture statements that describe the fearful condition of this world at the time of Christ's return. Instead of there being universal peace on the earth at the time of His coming, the Bible declares that the whole world will be engulfed in the most dreadful carnage of blood of all its history. Instead of there being a condition of universal righteousness, or, as the postmillennialists say, "a Christian world" at the time of our Lord's return, it will rather be a time of entrenched wickedness and awful unbelief.

Instead of there being a prevalence of high moral standards and good will among men at the time of Christ's coming, the Word of God says, "Knowing this also, that in the last days, perilous times shall come. For men shall be lovers of their own selves, covetous, boasters, proud, blasphemers, disobedient to parents, unthankful, unholy, without natural affection, truce breakers, false accusers, incontinent, fierce, despisers of those that are good, traitors, heady, highminded, lovers of pleasure more than lovers of God; having a form of godliness, but denying the power thereof," (2 Tim. 3:1-5). Take also the parable of the tares as given in the 13th chapter of Matthew:

"The kingdom of heaven is likened unto a man which sowed good seed in his field; but when the man slept, his enemy came and sowed tares among the wheat, and went his way. But when the blade was sprung up, and brought forth good fruit, then appeared the tares also. So the servants of the householder came and said unto him, Sir, didst thou not sow good seed in thy field? From whence then hath it tares? He said unto them, An enemy has done this. The servants said unto him, Wilt thou then that we go and gather them up? But he said, Nay: lest while ye gather up the tares, ye root up also the wheat with them. Let both grow together until the harvest: and in the time of the harvest I will say to the reapers, gather ye together first the tares, and bind them in bundles to burn them; but gather the wheat into my barn."

And, in order that there should be no mistake as to the meaning of the parable, Jesus gave the interpretation of it in these words:

"He that soweth the good seed is the Son of man; the field is the world; the good seed are the children of the Kingdom; but the tares are the children of the wicked one; the enemy that sowed them is the devil; the harvest is the *end of the world;* and the reapers are the angels. The Son of man shall send forth his angels, and they shall gather out of his kingdom all things that offend, and them which do iniquity, and shall cast them into a furnace of fire; there shall be wailing and gnashing of teeth. Then shall the rightous shine forth as the sun in the kingdom of their Father".

Here our Lord teaches plainly that the tares shall continue to grow with the wheat, and that the wicked shall continue to dwell with the righteous on this earth until Christ returns.

Christ taught the same truth in the parable of the net. He said: "The kingdom of heaven is like unto a net, that was cast into the sea, and gathered of every kind; which, when it was full, they drew to shore, and sat down, and gathered the good into vessels, but cast the bad away. So shall it be at the end of the age: the angels shall come forth and shall sever the wicked from among the just," (Matt. 13:47-49).

But the postmillennialists would say that Jesus did not know what He was talking about. They propose to eradicate all evil from the world, usher in a reign of universal good will among men, then, after a thousand years, if Christ does come at all, it will be for the purpose of pronouncing the race perfect. How diametrically opposed is this to all that the Bible teaches concerning the *exceeding sinfulness of men,* and *his hopelessness* to ever measure up to the divine standard. There never was a greater folly than the supposition that there could ever be a reign of universal righteousness on this earth until that day when "the Sun of righteousness shall arise with healing in His wings". There could be no more hopeless undertaking than to try to usher in a reign of universal peace; only the Prince of Peace Himself can do this.

Yes, the theory of postmillennialism is one of the greatest of heresies. It denies the plain teachings of the Bible. It is a philosophy that, at the very heart, is as antagonistic to Christian doctrine as any pagan philosophy, and more so, I think, because of its subtle character. It is a beautiful, Utopian, idealistic dream that *appears* to be Christian, but when examined in the light of the Word of God is found to be at enmity with the teachings and principles of Christianity.

It is evolutionary in nature. It declares the race to be morally and spiritually progressive, and promises an age when humanity shall be made perfect. It is humanistic. It glorifies and deifies man, and therefore, dethrones Christ. Any system that magnifies the achievements of man—dishonors God. Postmillennialism is the essence of modernism; in fact, it is the parent of modernism. This we do know: many modernists are postmillennialist, and we have never known of a modernist who is a pre-millennialist.

Briefly, now, we examine the new heresy of "amillennialism". As indicated earlier, this theory was developed recently by erstwhile postmillennialists. They realized the utter hopelessness of their position. But they would not accept the premillennial truth. They decided on the course of spiritualizing all the teaching on the subject. Everything was to have a figurative interpretation; nothing to be accepted as literal.

Accordingly, the passage on the millennium in Revelation 20 is not to be accepted in the plain and simple language in which the prophecy is given. The binding of Satan is only a symbol, they say. The "bottomless pit" into which Satan is cast is a mere figure of speech. The resurrection of the saints "before" the thousand years' reign of Christ is not accepted as literal. The kingdom of righteousness and peace under the personal, visible rule of Jesus Christ, is not literal; and, in fact, the period of time specified as one thousand years is not an actual, literal millennium, but only a figure of speech, they declare.

Most of these amillennialists run to the shelter of the so-called "historical" school; that is, the theory that those prophecies concerning the establishment of Christ's kingdom have *already* been fulfilled! But they differ among themselves: Some say that Christ's reign began on the day of His resurrection; some speculate that this "reign" began when Jesus was "seated at the right hand of God"; and others, that it began at the time of the fall of the Roman Empire. This theory proclaims the utterly fantastic claim that Christians are *now* "reigning" with Christ. Preposterous!

Thus we conclude that amillennialism is no improvement over postmillennialism. Both are extremely heretical teachings, a complete departure from the simple teachings of God's Word, and should therefore be shunned by all who seek the enlightenment of God's truth.

Christ's imminent return is revealed in many, many Scriptures. The Scriptural injunctions to "watch", "patiently wait", "look for", "pray for", "hasten", and "love" the day of His appearing have taken on a new meaning. To those who entertain the thought of the Lord's imminent return, the Bible is a new book, testimony is a joy, and sacrifice is the law of life. This mighty truth is blazing its way into the hearts of believers everywhere.

XII The Mystery of the Kingdom of Heaven

The Mystery of the Kingdom Of Heaven

This present age is characterized in Scripture as "the mystery of the kingdom of heaven." A mystery, not in the sense that it cannot be understood, but rather in the sense in that God's unusual and extraordinary dealings with men for *this* age were not revealed to the Old Testament saints.

Old Testament prophecies certainly revealed the coming of the Messiah to accomplish redemption by making a propitiatory sacrifice. Those Scriptures also revealed the future establishment of Christ's temporal kingdom through Israel. However, there was no revelation of what would occur on this earth between the time of Christ's offering for sin and the time of the establishment of His kingdom.

That period of time is called the dispensation of the grace of God, or the church age. It is frequently referred to in the New Testament as the mystery of the kingdom of heaven. Unknown to God's ancient people, but revealed through the Gospels and through the inspired interpretation of the Gospel by the Apostles.

It must be remembered that all the covenants of the Old Dispensation from the time of Abraham concerned the nation of Israel. The prophets emphasized that God's kingdom purposes, the fulfillment of His Theocracy, were centered in the Nation of Israel. The nature of that future kingdom was described in clear outline by Isaiah, Jeremiah, Ezekiel, Hosea, Daniel, Micah, and many others.

However, it was not until the time of the captivities that God undertook to reveal through Daniel certain time-periods which would mark the future years of Israel's place in God's dealings prior to the establishment of the millennial kingdom. I have previously called attention to those prophecies in Daniel which mark off a time period of 70 sevens of years, or 490 years. This period was to begin at the time of the decree of King Artaxerxes, authorizing the Jews to return, and rebuild Jerusalem. The first sixty-nine of these weeks of years, or 483 years was to terminate with the "cutting off of Messiah," or His rejection and crucifixion. That time-period is a matter of history. It was exactly 483 years from that well known date in history until the Lord Jesus was crucified outside that same city of Jerusalem.

Afterward, there would be another seven-year period, which we call Daniel's Seventieth Week, in which the Nation would occupy the central stage in the enactment of God's program on earth, prior to the establishment of the Millennial Kingdom. That period we know, from numerous other Scriptures, is to embrace the Great Tribulation period; and since this Great Tribulation period has not yet occurred, we know that there is an interval in human history separating the sixty-nine weeks, or 483 years, from the Seventieth Week, or seven years. That interval of time is not given, but we do know that it has already reached over a period of over nineteen hundred years. We do know that God's dealing with the Nation of Israel, so far as their kingdom program was concerned, was interrupted at the time of Christ's sacrifice, and that they have been "set aside" while the "mystery of the kingdom of heaven" is at work, during the course of this age. The revelation of this mystery is set forth in Acts 15:14, which reports the unveiling of the mystery which came from the Jerusalem council, and is declared to be God's purpose in this age to "visit the Gentiles" and to "take out a people for His name."

This "taking out of a people from among the Gentiles" constitutes God's program for this present age, and *this people* constitutes the church. We therefore refer to this period as the "church age." This age is the "mystery" period of the kingdom of heaven. The character of the mystery is described by Paul, in these words, from Col. 1:25-27: "Whereof I am made a minister, according to the dispensation of God which is given to me for you, to fulfill the word of God: even the mystery which hath been hid from ages and from generations, but now is made manifest to His saints: to whom God would make known what is the riches of the glory of this mystery among the Gentiles; which is Christ in you, the hope of glory."

So, it is crystal-clear that that which was a mystery before the coming of Christ, has now been revealed, and made known, in the church—the called-out ones from among the Gentiles. That mystery is declared to be "Christ in you, the hope of glory." The establishing of Christ's church, made up of individual believers, born again and indwelt by the Holy Spirit, is a great company of people, a heavenly people, who are to show forth the praises of God in Christ, world without end.

This, then, is the dispensation of the grace of God— a time period in the history of the world when God is manifesting the attributes of His grace, in such fashion as never before, in the forgiveness of sinners, and in their justification, through the finished work of Christ's atoning death; and in their complete redemption of both soul and body, to the praise of His glory. The supreme object of God in this unspeakable program of infinite mercy is stated in Ephesians 2:7, in these words: "That in the ages to come He might show forth the exceeding riches of His grace in His kindness toward us through Christ Jesus." And this Scripture indicates that God will con-

tinue throughout the ceaseless ages of eternity to reveal
to us the unfathomable mystery of His grace; not only
to reveal, but to display, to demonstrate—"that He might
show forth the exceeding riches of His grace."

Through the Gospel the veil of the mystery of the
kingdom of heaven is lifted, so that that which was
formerly unknown may now be known and understood.
Even as Paul declared, (1 Cor. 2:7), "We speak the wisdom of God in a mystery, even the hidden wisdom, which
God ordained before the world unto our glory." He goes
on to say that "Eye hath not seen, nor ear heard,
neither have entered into the heart of man, the things
which God hath prepared for them that love Him. . . ."
Now, mark the word: "But God hath revealed them unto
us by His Spirit: for the Spirit searcheth all things, yea,
the deep things of God." The context of this second
chapter of First Corinthians shows that the "mysteries
of the kingdom of heaven" are not mysteries to them who
believe, because the Holy Spirit who indwells born-again
believers interprets to us the things of God, truths which
are otherwise mysteries to the unbelieving world, and
truths which were unknown because unrevealed during
the Old Dispensation.

There are several elements of mystery, (ably set forth
by Dr. J. Dwight Pentecost): "The existence of this
present age, which was to interrupt God's established program with Israel, was a mystery (Matt. 13:11). That
Israel was to be blinded so that Gentiles might be brought
into relation to God was a mystery (Rom. 11:25). The
formulation of the church, made up of Jews and Gentiles
to form a body, was a mystery (Eph. 3:3-9; Col. 1:26-27;
Eph. 1:9; Rom. 16:25). The whole program of God that
results in salvation was called a mystery (1 Cor. 2:7).
The relation of Christ to men in redemption was called a
mystery (Col. 2:2; 4:3). The incarnation itself is called

a mystery (1 Tim. 3:16), not as to fact, but as to accomplishment. The development of evil unto its culmination in the man of sin (2 Thess. 2:7) and the development of the great apostate religious system (Rev. 17:5,7) both constitute that which was called a mystery. That there should be a new method by which God received men into His presence apart from death was a mystery (1 Cor. 15:51). These, then, constitute a major portion of God's program for the present age, which was not revealed in other ages, but is now known by revelation from God.''

The burden of my emphasis is that *this age* is the interval between Daniel's Sixty-ninth Week, and Seventieth Week—an interval which lasts from the time that Israel rejected the Messiah *until* the end of the church age, which will be terminated by the rapture, when God will again deal with Israel in judgment for a period of time described as Daniel's Seventieth Week, immediately prior to the establishment of Christ's Millennial Kingdom on this earth.

It must be emphasized, therefore, that God's work in this age is the gathering out of a people from among the Gentiles, from among all the nations of the earth, to constitute His spiritual body, the church of which Christ is the head. This "gathering out" process is accomplished through the preaching of the Gospel; and when the last soul is won, the last soul needed to constitute the body of Christ, the church (of born-again believers) will be snatched away from this earth. It is then that God will resume His dealings with Israel in judgment.

It is so very important that we have a clear perspective of this divine program, because we hear so much nowadays about the "building of God's kingdom on the earth" through the church. Such a fallacy is nowhere taught in the Scriptures. The purpose of the church is *not* to establish the kingdom of God on the earth. The purpose of the church is "to gather out a people" for God through the preaching of the Gospel, from among all nations. This is according to the specific terms of the Great Commission which our Lord gave to His church, in Matt. 28:18-20. When this work is consummated, the church will then become the Bride of Christ, and will be raptured for the heavenly nuptials, as described in the 19th chapter of Revelation.

The period of this present age is described by our Lord as the "mystery of the kingdom of heaven." How wonderful to have a part in God's great program for this age, to be an heir of God, and a joint-heir with the Lord Jesus Christ. The time is short. The evening shadows lengthen, as our age draws toward its close. "Watchman, what of the night?" Many of us will soon hear that glorious summons, "Behold, the Bridegroom cometh: go ye out to meet Him." "Even so, come Lord Jesus."

XIII   Christ's Coming for His Church

Christ's Coming for His Church

In His farewell discourse with His disciples, Jesus promised, "I go to prepare a place for you. And if I go and prepare a place for you, I will come again, and receive you unto Myself," (John 14:2,3).

Those words from the lips of Him who was the very incarnation of truth have formed the basis for the bright and blessed hope of God's children for almost two thousand years.

The personal return of our Lord: "I will come again," and for the purpose of receiving His people up into the mansions of glory: "And receive you unto Myself."

On the occasion of His ascension, the Heavenly messengers promised the awe-struck disciples who saw Him go away into Heaven, that "THIS SAME JESUS SHALL SO COME IN LIKE MANNER AS YE HAVE SEEN HIM GO INTO HEAVEN".

Likewise, under the inspiration of the Spirit, Paul promised that "the Lord Himself shall descend from Heaven with a shout, with the voice of the archangel, and with the trump of God."

And he said that all believers should look "for that blessed hope, the glorious appearing of the great God, even our Lord Jesus Christ," (Titus 2:13).

In like manner, James called upon the people to be patient, for "the coming of the Lord draweth nigh".

Jude says: "Behold, the Lord cometh," (Jude verse 14).

The inspired John, also, looked forward to this greatest of all events for the church, when he said, "Now are we the children of God, and it doth not yet appear what we shall be: but we know that WHEN HE SHALL APPEAR, we shall be like Him, for we shall see Him as He is,'' (1 John 3:2,3). And the whole of his prophecy of the last book of our Bible is called THE REVELATION (or ''unveiling'') OF JESUS CHRIST, and is occupied completely with the events of His coming again, clear to the final prayer of this book, ''Even so, come, Lord Jesus''.

We speak particularly, at this time, of His coming for His church. All students of prophecy are familiar with the two different phases of Christ's coming: first, to rapture the church; and, second, to reveal Himself to Israel, and forthwith to establish His kingdom. I believe these events will be separated by the space of Daniel's 70th week, or a period of at least seven years. The first phase of His coming, that is, His coming for His church, is imminent—it may occur at any moment.

It is well, I believe, to specify what is meant by ''the church''. It, of course, means but one thing: His ''called-out company of born-again believers''. I emphasize the qualification, ''born-again'' believers, for these only are members of the spiritual body of Christ. Mere professing Christians, or church members, according to the general usage of the term, are not necessarily members of the true body of Christ. There are millions in our churches today who have never been born again. Remember, Jesus said, ''Except a man be born again, he cannot see the kingdom of God.'' There must be a spiritual transformation, wrought by the power of God's Holy Spirit upon those who sincerely repent of sin, and believe wholly on Christ for salvation. Born-again Christians constitute the true spiritual, or mystical, body of Christ.

And it is this ''mystical body'' which is also called the Bride of Christ. This mystery is revealed in the Fifth chapter of Ephesians in a comparison of the conjugal relationship between husband and wife, and Christ and His church: "Husbands, love your wives, even as Christ loved the church, and gave Himself for it; that He might sanctify and cleanse it by the washing of water by the Word, that He might PRESENT IT TO HIMSELF a glorious church, not having spot or wrinkle, or any such thing; but that it should be holy and without blame." Then is added the word: "I speak concerning Christ and the church."

Again, in the 11th chapter of 2nd Corinthians, we read, "I have espoused you to one husband, that I may present you as a chaste virgin to Christ".

The tremendous event of this heavenly marriage is described in the 19th chapter of Revelation. Here the church, the Bride, has "made herself ready", and is received by Christ, the Great Bridegroom. Mark the words in verses 7 to 10: "Let us be glad and rejoice, and give honor to Him: for the marriage of the Lamb is come, and His wife hath made herself ready. And to her was granted that she should be arrayed in fine linen, clean and white: for the fine linen is the righteousness (righteous deeds) of the saints. And he saith unto me, Write, Blessed are they which are called unto the marriage supper of the Lamb. And he saith unto me, These are the true sayings of God."

This heavenly marriage is therefore the climax of the blessed event of our Lord's return for His church. It was emphasized by our Lord in the parable of the ten virgins. Five of the virgins were ready when they heard the blessed summons, "Behold, the bridegroom cometh, go ye out to meet Him . . . and they that were ready, went in with Him to the marriage; and the door was shut". Then, Jesus added that earnest word of admonition: "Watch therefore, for ye know neither the day nor the hour wherein the Son of man cometh."

The Apostle Paul, writing under the inspiration of God to the Thessalonian Christians, presented the prophetic picture of the great events which are to occur at the mo-

ment of our Lord's return for His people. In chapter 4
of the First epistle to the Thessalonians, he comforted
those whose loved ones had been snatched away by the
hand of death. He said, concerning those whose bodies
were sleeping in the graves, that the living saints should
not sorrow as those who have no hope:

> "For if we believe that Jesus died and rose again,
> even so them also which sleep in Jesus will God bring
> with Him. For this we say unto you, by the word of
> the Lord, that we which are alive and remain unto
> the coming of the Lord shall not precede them which
> are asleep (in the graves). For the Lord Himself
> shall descend from Heaven, with a shout, with the
> voice of the archangel, and with the trump of God;
> and the dead in Christ shall rise first: then we which
> are alive and remain shall be caught up"—(there is
> the glorious rapture of the church)—"caught up to-
> gether with them in the clouds, to meet the Lord in
> the air: and so shall we ever be with the Lord. Where-
> fore comfort one another with these words."

Here we have revealed that in that stupendous moment,
described as occurring "in the twinkling of an eye", first
of all, the resurrection of all who have died in the faith—
and this includes both the Old Testament saints and the
New Testament saints. The bodies of believers of all generations of time shall be instantly snatched from their
graves, whether those graves be in the ground, or in the
waters, all shall come forth. This is the first resurrection,
and only the saints are included. Not until the second
resurrection will the bodies of the unregenerate be resurrected.

Today, as you and I contemplate that wonderful occasion, we are doubtless thinking of some of our dear ones
who have gone on to be with the Lord. We took their
earthly remains out to the silent city of the dead, and the

lifeless form was lowered into the new-made grave. A few
spades of clay filled up the empty space, and then we left
some flowers there, and watered them with our burning
tears, and walked slowly away, awaiting the morning of
the resurrection. Oh, my dear friends, fellow-heirs of the
promises of God, we have in this prophetic Scripture the
assurance of that glad day when those graves shall be
instantly opened, and the precious forms of our dear ones
shall come forth in glorified bodies, and we shall see them
again!

This prophecy declares that we who remain until the
coming of the Lord shall not precede these dead saints
to glory; we shall have no advantage over them just
because we happen to be here when the Lord comes. It is
as if the good hand of our God holds us back for a breath-
taking second; and it is as if we might hear Him say,
"Now, just wait a moment, you cannot go up into glory
until these in the graves are all resurrected . . . just wait
a moment, and you will all come up together"!

For in the midst of that greatest moment of eternity,
this prophecy declares that we shall all be glorified, and
instantly snatched away from this earth in the rapture:
"Then we which are alive and remain shall be caught up
. . ." This is the big event to which we look forward.
This is the event of which the Apostle speaks in Titus 2:13,
in these words: "Looking for that blessed hope, the glorious appearing of the great God, even our Saviour Jesus
Christ."

This is the event which is spoken of in the 15th chapter
of First Corinthians, in these majestic words: "Behold, I
show you a mystery: we shall not all sleep, but we shall
all be changed, IN A MOMENT, IN THE TWINKLING
OF AN EYE, at the last trump: for the trumpet shall
sound, and the dead shall be raised incorruptible, and we
shall be changed. For this corruptible must put on incor-
ruption, and this mortal must put on immortality . . .

Then shall be brought to pass the saying that is written, Death is swallowed up in victory . . .''

Now, back to the Thessalonian passage: ''Then we which are alive shall be caught up—(mark the words)—TOGETHER WITH THEM IN THE CLOUDS.'' There is the picture of the reunion. We shall not go to heaven apart from them, and they shall not go apart from us, praise God! Both the dead and the living saints shall be raptured simultaneously—''together with them''. Oh, what a day of blessedness that will be. Think of it! Think of meeting all our dear ones who have died in the faith; think of meeting them all—everyone of them—on the morning of the resurrection. Not one will be missing. ''Together with them,'' we shall sail away through the clouds. Talk about a flight through outer space; talk about a flight to the moon; or to Mars, or Jupiter, or Saturn—nothing shall compare with that glorious flight through infinite space, even into Heaven itself!

For we are promised that ''together with them in the clouds'' WE SHALL MEET THE LORD IN THE AIR. We shall not see the face of the Great Bridegroom until we get up into the air. In that moment, beloved, we shall forget every care we have ever known; every cross, every heartache, every trial—all these will vanish, and all tears shall be wiped away in that glad moment when we meet the Lord in the air!

And, then, it is added, ''AND SO SHALL WE EVER BE WITH THE LORD''. At that moment shall begin for us that unending day of peace and Heavenly blessedness. This is the heritage of the people of God.

My friend, will you be in that company of the redeemed of God? You may be—you can be. The invitation is for you today: ''Whosoever shall call upon the name of the Lord shall be saved.'' ''As many as received Him, to them gave He power to become the children of God, even to them that believe on His name.''

XIV Two Pivotal Judgments of the Future

Two Pivotal Judgments of the Future

Today we examine from the prophetic Scriptures two pivotal judgments. I qualify these judgments as *pivotal* because there are several other judgments; such as, the judgments on Israel, the judgment of sin on the cross, and the judgment of the nations at our Lord's second advent.

The two outstanding judgments are (1) The Judgment Seat of Christ, and (2) The Judgment of the Great White Throne. The first has to do with believers, and occurs after the rapture. The second is concerned only with unbelievers, and occurs more than one thousand years later, following the Millennium. Before examining the nature of these two pivotal judgments, it is important that we give attention, at least briefly, to the *two* resurrections, for these are preludes to the two judgments.

No teaching in the Scriptures is more positively accented than that all the dead will be raised. It is a doctrine which is subscribed to in confessions of faith of all denominations—Protestant, Catholic, and Jewish. There has been little controversy over the solid Scriptural teaching of a resurrection.

However, many who are not acquainted with the Scriptures do not realize that there are to be *two* resurrections. All the dead are not to come forth on the same occasion, such as a so-called *general* resurrection. These resurrections are described in the 20th chapter of Revelation as the *first* resurrection, and the *second* resurrection. And these are to be separated by the space of more than one thousand years.

These two resurrections are spoken of in the Scriptures as the resurrection of the *just,* and the resurrection of the unjust; also, as the "resurrection of life" and the "resurrection of damnation". Our Lord spoke thus concerning these resurrections: "Marvel not at this: for the hour is coming, in which all that are in the graves shall hear His voice, and shall come forth; they that have done good, unto the resurrection of life; and they that have done evil, unto the resurrection of damnation," (John 5:28,29).

Again, our Lord distinguished this first resurrection in these words: "When thou makest a feast, call the poor, the maimed, the lame, the blind: and thou shalt be blest: for thou shalt be recompensed *at the resurrection of the just,*" (Luke 14:13,14).

Speaking of the first resurrection, the Apostle Paul stated in First Corinthians 15: "As in Adam all die, even so in Christ shall all be made alive. But every man in his own order; Christ the first-fruits, afterward, they that are Christ's at His coming." Again, he reminded the Thessalonian Christians, as he wrote under the inspiration of the Spirit, that "the dead in Christ shall rise *first*". This fact is clearly taught, also, in Philippians 3:11.

The time which intervenes between the first and the second resurrections is clearly stated in Revelation 20. Listen to the Word of God:

> "And I saw thrones, and they that sat upon them, and judgment was given unto them: and I saw the souls of them that were beheaded for the witness of Jesus, and for the Word of God, and which had not worshipped the Beast, neither his image, neither had received his mark upon their foreheads, or in their hands; and *they lived and reigned with Christ a thousand years.* But the REST OF THE DEAD lived not again until the thousands years were finished. This is the FIRST RESURRECTION. Blessed and holy

is he that hath part in the FIRST RESURRECTION;
on such the second death hath no power, but they
shall be priests unto God and of Christ, and shall reign
with Him a thousand years.''

Then the verses which follow describe the second resurrection, that is, the resurrection of the wicked, and the
judgment of the Great White Throne, which we shall examine presently. Before leaving this point, however, it is
important to remember that the first resurrection is in at
least three stages.

Paul describes the resurrection of Christ as ''the first-
fruits'' of the resurrection. And we must remember that
on that wonderful occasion, there was also a partial resurrection of the saints, as Matthew reports: ''And the
graves were opened; and many bodies of the saints which
slept arose, and came out of the graves *after His resurrection,* and went into the holy city and appeared unto
many,'' (Matt. 27:52, 53).

The second stage of the *first* resurrection will be when
Jesus comes for His church, evidently preceding the Great
Tribulation. And the third and final stage of the first
resurrection will occur at the end of the Tribulation period,
and will include those who refused to worship the Beast.
(Rev. 20.)

But the *second* resurrection is one single event. The
wicked dead of all generations from the time of Adam
shall be in that company, coming forth from their graves.

We are now prepared to view the two judgment scenes.
The first of these, as already stated, is the Judgment Seat
of Christ. It shall occur in the heavens. The subjects
shall be the saints of God, both they of the first resurrection and those ''who are alive and remain unto the coming
of the Lord,'' who shall be caught up in the rapture. The
period of this judgment shall begin after the rapture, and
may well extend over the period of Daniel's Seventieth

Week, or seven years, until the tribulation saints are raptured.

But, it is important to know the reason for the judgment
seat of Christ. What are the issues involved? What is
the basis of this judgment of the redeemed of God? Is
there to be a determination as to whether they are to be
accepted? No! They have already been accepted. They
would not be in that glorified company if they were not
accepted. Then, are they to be punished because of their
sins? No! That would be impossible. The sins of all
believers have been judged on the cross. The Lord Jesus
Christ assumed our guilt, and was condemned (judged) in
our place, and bore the full penalty, for time and eternity,
for every sin we have committed.

This is a precious truth to God's people, and of tremendous importance. Christ's redeeming sacrifice brings
to the trusting sinner both pardon and justification. "Who
His Own Self bare our sins in His Own body on the tree."
The deep meaning of the atonement is that "the Lord
hath laid on Him the iniquity of us all;" that "Christ died
for our sins;" that "the blood of Jesus Christ cleanseth us
from all sin". And, in this transaction, God's perfect
righteousness is imputed to us who believe (placed over
to our credit): "For He hath made Him to be sin for us,
Who knew no sin; that we might be made the righteousness of God in Him," (2 Cor. 5:21).

The sinner is acquitted from all guilt when he trusts
Christ, and the believer is forever justified, and cannot
therefore be judged again with respect to sin: "There is
therefore now no condemnation (judgment) to them that
are in Christ Jesus," (Rom. 8:1). Even as our Lord also
said, the believer "shall not come into judgment, but is
passed from death unto life." And, He said: "Their sins
and iniquities I will remember no more," (Heb. 10:17).

It is therefore crystal-clear that the sin question, having been fully and finally settled at the cross, will not be

considered at the judgment seat of Christ, before which
seat the saints shall stand. It is to be a judgment of the
believer's work. Every *work* shall come into judgment.
The life, the walk, the conversation, the works of Christians must be reviewed by the Lord, and rewarded accordingly.

"For we must all appear before the judgment seat of
Christ; that every one may receive the things done in his
body, according to that he hath done, whether it be good
or bad," (2 Cor. 5:10). Again, we read in Romans 14:10:
"For we shall all stand before the judgment seat of
Christ." The context of both these Scriptures make it
plain that only believers are included at this particular
judgment—the judgment seat of Christ.

The basis on which our works are judged is pointed out
in the third chapter of First Corinthians, in these words:

"For other foundation can no man lay than that
is laid, which is Christ Jesus. Now if any man build
upon this foundation gold, silver, precious stones,
wood, hay stubble; every man's work shall be made
manifest; for the day shall declare it, because it shall
be revealed by fire; and the fire shall try *every man's
work* of what sort it is. If any man's work abide
which he hath built thereupon, he shall *receive a reward.* If any man's work shall be burned, he shall
suffer loss: but *he himself* shall be saved; yet so as
by fire."

This particular judgment is referred to by our Lord,
Who said, "Behold, I come quickly; and *My reward* is with
Me, to give every man according as his work shall be,"
(Rev. 22:12).

This judgment seat of Christ was in the mind of the
beloved Paul, who wrote: "Henceforth, there is laid up
for me a crown of righteousness, which the Lord, the

righteous *judge,* shall give me at that day: and not to me only, but unto all them that love His appearing,'' (2 Tim. 4:8).

So, we see that this judgment following the *first* resurrection is something completely different from the judgment which follows the thousand years, namely, the judgment of the Great White Throne.

It is well that we note some contrasting facts respecting these two central judgments of the future:

As to time, the Judgment Seat of Christ will occur before the Millennium. The final Judgment will occur after the Millennium.

As to place, the Judgment Seat of Christ will be in the heavens. The final judgment will be at the Great White Throne.

As to subjects, only the saints will be present at the Judgement Seat of Christ. Only unbelievers and the unregenerate will be present at the Great White Throne.

As to the basis of judgment, at the Judgment Seat of Christ, believers will be judged for their works, or according to their faithfulness. At the Great White Throne, the wicked will be judged because of their sins.

As to the result of the judgment, at the Judgment Seat of Christ believers will be rewarded, or will suffer loss, in relation to the measure of their faithfulness; yet, even the unfaithful will not be condemned, but will be saved ''yet so as by fire''. At the Great White Throne where no one's name is found in the Lamb's book of life all are condemned, and shall go away into everlasting punishment.

To the believers at the Judgment Seat of Christ will be given the welcome plaudit, ''Enter thou into the joy of thy Lord.'' To the unbelievers at the judgment of the Great White Throne, will be the Divine verdict, ''Depart, ye cursed, into everlasting fire, prepared for the devil and his angels . . . I never knew you.''

There will be no appeal from that verdict by the Supreme Court of the Universe. The judgment is according to the justice and righteousness of God, and is therefore final.

We now take a look at this final judgment scene, described in the 20th chapter of Revelation. We are told that "when the thousand years have expired, Satan shall be loosed out of his prison," where he has been held captive in a place called "the bottomless pit". It is from this prison that he shall be "loosed", evidently for only a little season, and he shall "go out to deceive the nations which are in the four corners of the earth, Gog and Magog, to gather them together to battle," against Christ, the King of the earth. Mark the fact that this is to occur at the end of the millennial kingdom.

It is indeed a pitiful story, and a sad anticlimax to the glorious Millennium. But it is the repetition of the old story of Satanic hatred against God, and of man's frailty and disposition to rebel against the will of God. A thousand years in the bottomless pit makes Satan no better; while a thousand years under the personal reign of Christ leaves man yet at enmity with God.

But a madder attempt was never made than this final rebellion against the Son of God, for it is the march of doom, a march into the jaws of death and into the mouth of hell. One brief sentence tells the fateful, fearful story: "And fire came down from heaven and destroyed them." However, the destruction was not annihilation, as we are presently to see, for they are raised from the dead to appear with all the rest of the sinners of all ages before the Judgment. And we are told that the devil is then to be cast into the lake of fire and brimstone, the place originally prepared for him and for his angels.

And, now, the Great White Throne appears. What solemn, what awful words are used to describe the Occupant of that Throne! "And I saw a great white throne, and

Him that sat on it from whose face the earth and the heaven fled away; and there was found no place for them," (vs. 11). It is none other than the Son of God! The same Son of God Who has existed eternally with the Father; the same Son Who in due time identified Himself with our race, and was born in Bethlehem's manger; Who grew up at Nazareth, and Who ministered to the needs of this poor world, both physically and spiritually, as none ever ministered, and Who offered Himself up as a substitutionary sacrifice for our sins, Who was despised and rejected, and crucified by the world; the same One Who rose from the dead, and after forty days ascended to the Father; the same One Who appears there now as our Priest and Intercessor; the same One Who is coming to call the true Church to heaven; the same One Who will reign personally as King of kings, as the Sun of righteousness for a thousand years—Ah, let the earth tremble!—It is the Son of God Who is to occupy that judgment throne!

"And I saw the dead, small and great, stand before God." All the wicked dead of all ages and generations, all who have resisted the will of God, and have not accepted Him; the great, the rich, the poor, the educated, the illiterate, the renown, the unknown, all nationalities, all tongues, all colors—ALL.

The sea and the grave will give up the bodies; hades will give up the spirits. What a sea of faces will be gathered about that great judgment throne!

"And the books were opened and another book was opened, which is the book of life." So there will be at least two sets of books from which these will be judged. First, there will be *books* opened that day that record all the deeds of evil of every soul in that company—every guilty thought, every evil purpose, every wrong act, every sinful deed, every unclean word—all will be laid bare, and the conscience of men will attest to the truth of that divine record! Every evil act will be traced directly to its source. Then, there will be the Bible, the Word of God. For Jesus said that both the words of Moses and His own words would judge them at that day.

And we are told that *"another book," the book of life* will be opened. But why? Simply because there will be some in that great company who will seek to plead their self-righteousness and their beneficence and their morality; so that the book of life on which the names of all the redeemed of God are recorded shall be presented to show that their names are not written thereon. "Then shall the King say, 'Depart from Me, ye cursed, into everlasting fire, prepared for the devil and his angels,' for 'I never knew you'!" We are not told of a single one whose name was found on the book of life. For all the redeemed are already resurrected, and in heaven, at the time of this awful assize.

"Every man was judged according to his works." There will be just graduations of punishment, as well as there will be just graduations of rewards for the righteous. But everyone will be judged according to the sins committed and according to the light rejected.

As death is the separation of the spirit from the body, so the second death will be the eternal separation of both soul and body from God. And the eternal abode will be the same lake of fire into which the Devil is cast. The destination is hell for every sinner not under the blood of Christ. Some want to assume that the final hell will not be literal fire and brimstone, but there is nowhere in God's Word any authority for such an assumption. But suppose that "fire" is, or should be only a figure of speech, as such it would be a figure of the real thing, and doubtless the real thing is worse than the figure that represents it. And if hell be worse than it is depicted here, then, God deliver any who are in danger of experiencing it.

Oh, my unsaved friend, you do not have to go to that awful place of unending, perpetual despair and suffering, for it is written that God "is not willing that any should perish, but that all should come to repentance". Today I remind you that you are still living in the day of grace, and the overtures of God's everlasting mercies are extended to you. There is mercy and pardon and justification for every sinner through the crucified and risen Redeemer. Today He bids you come to Him for salvation: "Behold, I stand at the door and knock; if any man hear My voice, *and open the door*—(the door of your heart)—I will come in to him, and will sup with him, and he with Me," (Rev. 3:20). And He said, "Him that cometh unto Me I will in no wise cast out."

Oh, today, "if you hear His voice, harden not your heart." "Whosoever shall call upon the name of the Lord shall be saved."

XV The Great Apostasy

The Great Apostasy

"There shall be false teachers among you, who privily shall bring in damnable heresies, even denying the Lord that bought them, and bring upon themselves swift destruction," 2 Pet. 2:1.

"For there are certain men crept in unawares, who were before of old ordained unto this condemnation, ungodly men, turning the grace of our God into lasciviousness, and denying the only Lord God, and our Lord Jesus Christ," Jude 4.

"There be some that would trouble you who would pervert the Gospel of Christ. But though we, or an angel from heaven, preach any other gospel unto you than that which we have preached unto you, let him be accursed," Gal. 1:7,8.

These Scriptures speak of the great apostasy, the falling away from the true faith to a false gospel, which began to be manifested in the first century, but which according to the clear word of prophecy is to sweep over the professing church at the end of this present age.

Every informed, Scripture-enlightened believer is familiar with this system of unbelief, this *perverted* gospel. In our own generation this dreadful apostasy has swept in like a flood. Its aggressive promoters are the religious liberals, the proponents of Modernism. God describes them as "ungodly men" who have "crept in unawares". Their assault is subtle, their method of approach is cunning deception. Their doom is pronounced in these, and many other Scriptures. If we are to know how close we are to the end of the age, we must examine the nature of this Satanic movement.

Modernism is that form of doctrine which, though it claims to be Christian, and parades under the guise of scholarship, is a complete perversion of Bible teachings.

It is called modernism, not because it is a modern interpretation of Christian theology, because in this respect it is not at all modern. Its fallacious assaults of Christian doctrine are as old as the human race, having its origin in the Garden of Eden when first Satan called in question and challenged the Word of God. Through all the centuries, Satan's emissaries have sought to pervert the truth by propounding a false interpretation of every single doctrine of the Bible.

But it is called modernism because of its modern *method of assault*. Heretofore, Satan's principal method of attacking Christianity has been from without the church. He has used atheists, agnostics, and infidels, and skeptics of every other brand to hammer away at the precious doctrines of our faith. There were the Voltaires and the Tom Paines and the Bob Ingersolls, who in their day, delivered relentless blows against God's Word. But when Satan could not succeed in his effort to overthrow Christianity by those means, he devised another strategy. He changed his *modus operandi*. He decided to do the Trojan Horse act—get into the church with his infidelity and bore from within.

Shortly after the turn of the present century, it began to be popular for men to stand in the pulpits of our churches, and in the guise of so-called scholarship, offer new interpretations on the doctrines of historic Christianity. These false interpretations which they had imbibed in the infidel schools where they studied their theology were such, in effect, as to completely repudiate the Christian faith. In other words, the Voltaires and the Tom Paines and the Bob Ingersolls moved into the churches, where, in the garb of Christian ministers, they could do their most deadly and most damning work of uprooting the faith of the people.

Because the protest of true Christian believers was not strong enough to halt this insidious assault on the Word of God, the movement grew and spread very rapidly. Soon it was discovered that most of the old-line theological seminaries had become, in reality, "cemeteries" where the Christian faith was buried, and where the so-called higher criticism became enthroned. And many of the historic churches of America, in turn, erstwhile pillars of orthodoxy, were captured by these liberals, so that they became breeding places for the development of modernism.

On the heels of this movement, there came into being a powerful ecclesiastical machine, falsely named the Federal Council of Churches of Christ in America. It was never a representative body, although it loudly and vigorously claimed to be. No delegate or official to that body was ever elected by the churches. Its officers always were chosen by a self-appointed group of ecclesiastics, many of whom do not believe the Bible to be the Word of God. It is now called the National Council of Churches.

Most of the leaders, if not all, of the National Council of Churches of Christ in America, so-called, have repudiated such doctrines of historic Christianity as the verbal inspiration of the Bible, the absolute deity of Christ, His virgin birth, His vicarious atonement, His bodily resurrection, and the precious truth of His second coming. They have kicked out the back door the old-fashioned doctrines of sin, and judgment, and hell.

In the place of these doctrines of historic Christianity, these modernists, parading under the false guise of the "National Council of Churches of Christ" have substituted the social gospel, which in reality is pure socialism, or "social collectivism." More than one Congressional investigation has found the NCCCA to be sympathetic toward Communism. They preached a false pacifism before and during the war. Many of these men are today in various "Communist front" organizations.

Now, they are doing everything in their power to indoctrinate the churches with their infidelistic philosophies. It is the duty of every true Christian minister, (and, thank God, there are many), to sound the alarm against the inroads of this Satanic philosophy. My own conviction is, that it is the movement of antichrist, and that, in time, when they have completed their efforts toward the organization a world ecumenical system, you will find them in league with the Communists. That is the direction toward which they are heading. Today their slogan is "peaceful co-existence with the Communists".

All of this is in line with the theory that Communism is the substitute for historic Christianity. Having repudiated the basic, fundamental tenets and doctrines of the Christian faith, it is but the natural, logical thing to turn to the atheistic system of Communism.

God's people must be warned against this pernicious system. Beware of the Bible-denying, faith-destroying philosophy of modernism. Flee from the seducive snares of the men who are, today, in the guise of Christian ordinances and ceremony, trying to make shipwreck of the precious doctrines of our faith. Shun those whose vain and meaningless shibboleths can serve no purpose but to spread unbelief and bring a reproach upon the name and person of Christ.

The central message of the Gospel of the grace of God is declared in the Epistle to the Galatians, namely, that "Christ gave Himself for our sins, that He might deliver us from the present evil world, according to the will of God and our Father," (1:4). God's purpose in this age is to redeem from the powers of darkness every son and daughter of Adam's race who will enter into the overtures of His everlasting mercy. The one basis for our redemption is Christ's sin offering, His own death on the cross. The credential of our hope is in the living Christ who rose from the dead.

The business of the church of Christ is to proclaim this message of redemption to a lost world. It is not the church's mission to "Christianize the social order", nor to try to control the political life of the world. Nor is it the mission of the church "to establish the kingdom of God on earth". The church's specific mission is set forth in the Great Commission, (Matt. 28-18-20).

God's redeemed people, who have been enlightened concerning the truth of God, converted, born again, regenerated, transformed, made children of God through faith in Jesus Christ, are responsible to Christ the Head of the church for carrying forward His program of redemption. A "peculiar people" commissioned with a particular task. As the representatives of Christ, we have been commanded to spread abroad the "good news" of heaven—to witness, testify, win souls, declare the Gospel of the grace of God to the uttermost part of the earth.

The evangelical message proclaims a divine Saviour who identified Himself with our race by His incarnation. Co-existent with the Father, He is the eternal Son of God; and born of the virgin Mary He became also the Son of Man.

This message declares that He lived a perfect life, utterly without sin; and that in His perfection He offered Himself in death as our substitutionary sacrifice for sin. Hence, we have a perfect Saviour.

This message proclaims His resurrection from the dead. Thus we have, not a dead Saviour, but a living Saviour, who is able to guarantee complete and eternal justification for every son and daughter of Adam's race who will look to Him.

This Gospel proclaims that Christ, as our living Saviour, is also our ever-faithful High Priest who continually represents His people to God. And what is more, this message of the evangel proclaims that "this same Jesus" shall return for His people, and that He shall thereafter establish His kingdom of righteousness and peace on this earth.

This is the evangelical message to be heralded by the church of Christ, and by every child of God. This is the primary business of the church. To introduce men to the Saviour must, therefore, be the first concern of every born-again soul. For this purpose we are to live, and labor and toil and sacrifice, and if need be, die.

We are under a commission and we are under a Captain. We take orders from the Son of God. No man is a disciple of Jesus who has not come under the Lordship of Christ. If you are unwilling to take orders, and execute orders from Christ, as your Lord, you are *not* one of His disciples.

Now, what is the matter with the church today? We know full well that the church is not fulfilling the Great Commission of Christ. Somewhere along the way a different concept has been set up. Somewhere there has entered in a shift of emphasis. There is the idea that the church is merely a betterment agency in the world. There is the idea that Christ is the head of the church *only* in the sense that He established it 1900 years ago . . . He is seldom thought of as the active, living head of the church today, in vital union with the institution which He established.

The matter of the New Birth as a prerequisite to membership in the church is thought of by many in a fantastic or a figurative way. Many people join churches today without ever reading a confession of faith, or without ever hearing a doctrinal sermon. One joins a church much the same way as one joins a club or an ethical society. There is the idea that one's membership in that church might make him a better person, a more worthwhile citizen.

The matter of how to be saved from sin is relegated as unimportant. Understanding the meaning of redemption is not necessary. The requirements of discipleship are given little consideration. The supernatural work of grace is overlooked. The indwelling Christ in the hearts of believers to produce their joy and peace is seldom preached.

The fellowship of the Holy Spirit, giving the child of God victory and power, and producing the fruit of the Spirit is an almost unheard-of doctrine. What we have left in modern theology is a "salvation-by-works" philosophy.

If salvation is secured by works of righteousness; if the goal is to merely produce ethical standards, then, it is needless to say, there is no place left for the preaching and teaching of the great basic, bedrock doctrines of redemption as they are revealed in the New Testament. The one is antagonistic to the other.

This shift of emphasis is not new. It began during the first generation of Christianity. The Apostle Paul branded it as a complete departure from the Gospel of Christ, and referred to it as "*another* Gospel". He warned Christians concerning this false system of theology. This Satanic cult had made inroad in the churches of Galatia. Concerning it, Paul said:

"I marvel that ye are so soon removed from Him that called you into the grace of Christ unto another Gospel: which is not another; but there be some that trouble you, and would pervert the Gospel of Christ."

Mark this fact well. Paul calls this shifted emphasis a "perversion" of the true Gospel. And, he lays the blame where it belongs, namely on the false teachers. He charges that they deliberately set out to "pervert" or corrupt the Gospel of Christ. They themselves had rejected the great doctrines of redemption, and had set out to sabotage the Gospel of a crucified and risen Redeemer.

Now, mark well the condemnation that is pronounced upon these religious liberals, these agents of Satan. Listen to the Word of God:

"But though we, or an angel from heaven, preach any other gospel unto you than that which we have preached unto you, let him be accursed."

And this severe denunciation is repeated in the next verses for double emphasis. God says here that those who pervert the Gospel of Christ will go to hell. "Let him be accursed!" Let him be forever condemned! It is a serious thing to tamper with the Word of the living God. To purchase our redemption it cost the Son of God His precious blood. All the wisdom of God, and all the justice of God, and all the mercy of God, and all the love of God were combined in this greatest transaction of the ages; and for men to despise that which God has designed, and seek to teach others to turn away from it, and to show contempt for it—I tell you, there remains nothing but the fiery indignation of a holy and righteous God against such men.

Now, let us examine this "perverted Gospel", the product of these Satanic false teachers. X-ray it, and you will find it to be the so-called "social gospel" which is stealthily advocated by the modernists today. The ecumenical movement is seeking today to control all the churches, and to accomplish on a world-wide scale the complete perversion of the Gospel of Christ. The social gospel which they advocate is "another gospel," which is not the Gospel of Christ.

In order, now, that we might have a clear picture of the difference between the Gospel of Christ and this Karl Marx social gospel, it will be well that we note some striking contrasts:

The Gospel of Christ aims to transform individuals by regeneration of the Spirit. The "social gospel" aims to improve society through the "human betterment" program.

The Gospel of Christ is the message of blood redemption for lost sinners. The "social gospel" is the message of economic and social reform for a world in spiritual darkness.

The Gospel of Christ has to do with spiritual concepts. The "social gospel" has to do with materialism.

The Gospel of Christ brings saved sinners into the brotherhood of the church. The "social gospel" aims to bring all men into the brotherhood of a socialistic state.

The Gospel of Christ offers the only hope to a lost world. The "social gospel" offers a false hope to a corrupt social order.

The Gospel of Christ is supernatural and is by faith. The "social gospel" proposes salvation by human agencies and by works. The former is of divine origin; the latter of human origin.

The Gospel of Christ proclaims "Christ lifted up" for sinners. The "social gospel" advocates merely an attempt to "uplift humanity".

The Gospel of Christ saves people for heaven. The "social gospel" aims only to help people live on this earth.

The "social gospel" is for *time* only. The Gospel of Christ is for time and eternity. The "social gospel" people look for a millennium by way "human betterment". Bible Gospel believers look for the millennium by way of Christ's personal and glorious return.

If the "social gospel" will save the world, then Christ died in vain! If human reformation is the hope of the world, then it is useless to preach individual spiritual regeneration based on Christ's blood redemption!

Now, this "social gospel" ecumenical movement has its political implications. Its advocates have a *definite end in view*. Their aim is on record. It is a far-reaching plan. What it adds up to, politically, is a social collectivism. If adopted in our nation it would completely subvert our form of government. There would be nothing left of our free enterprise system. The individual would be subservient to the state. And the state would be controlled by this ecclesiastical octopus. No individual could express independent convictions.

All would have to conform to that so-called church system, which, their leaders presumptuously call "the kingdom of God" on earth. In other words, God's program as set forth in the prophetic word must be set aside. The Lord Jesus Christ is not to return, as He and all the prophets and apostles promised—No, no. This apostate system of social collectivism must take its place!

Let God's people beware of this apostate ecumenical system. Beware of the voice of Modernism, for it is the spirit of Antichrist.

These apostate religious leaders were described by Jude in these appropriate words:

"Their mouth speaketh great swelling words, having men's persons in admiration because of advantage. But, beloved, remember ye the words which were spoken before of the apostles of our Lord Jesus Christ: how that they told you there should be mockers in the last time, who should walk after their own ungodly lusts. These be they that separate themselves, sensual, having not the Spirit." Jude 16-19.

Peter also delivered a terrific indictment against this cult of false teachers, (2 Pet. 2) who "beguile unstable souls". They are described as being "presumptuous, self-willed," and "not afraid to speak evil of dignities". He said, "They speak evil of the things they understand not, and shall utterly perish in their own corruption: and shall receive the reward of unrighteousness". Their doom is pronounced:

"These are wells without water, clouds that are carried with a tempest: to whom the mist of darkness is reserved forever . . . They speak great swelling words of vanity . . . they allure through the lusts of the flesh . . . They promise liberty while they themselves are the servants of corruption . . . For it had been better for them not to have known the way of righteousness, than, after they have known it, to turn from the holy commandment delivered unto them."

The great apostasy is the sure harbinger of the soon coming of our Lord. The clouds of unbelief and infidelity will grow darker until the Antichrist appears: "Let no man deceive you by any means: for that day shall not come, except there come a falling away first, and that man of sin be revealed, the son of perdition," 2 Thess. 2:3.

XVI Other Signs of His Soon Return

Other Signs of His Soon Return

In addition to the signs of our Lord's return mentioned in previous chapters, let us consider some timely reminders that we are rapidly reaching the end of the present age: some of these signs shall be more fully manifest during the Tribulation period, but already they are in evidence: **"Distress of nations with perplexity."**

Most timely is the revelation in Luke 21:24-27. Our Lord spoke of the end of "the times of the Gentiles", and said there should be upon the earth "distress of nations, with perplexity; the sea and the waves roaring; men's hearts failing them for fear, and for looking after those things which are coming on the earth: for the powers of heaven shall be shaken." Concerning those days God had spoken through the prophet Haggai five hundred years earlier, in these words: "I will shake all nations," (Hag. 2:6,7).

In our day, nations are striving, not so much for political position, as for *economic survival*. The result is the surrender of their absolute sovereignty for the advantage of consolidation with other nations. The outgrowth is confederations of nations, with increased tensions, issuing in "distress" and "perplexity".

This chaotic imbalance of power, resulting from the "shaking up of the nations" leads naturally to the "wars and rumors of wars" when "nation shall rise against nation, and kingdom against kingdom". There are weapons today—nuclear, chemical, and biological, besides the intercontinental ballistic missiles—that when unleashed will destroy the world, except for divine intervention.

"Famines and pestilences."

In answer to the disciples' question, "when shall these things be? and what shall be the sign of Thy coming, and of the end of the world?" (Matt. 24), our Lord mentioned among other things that "famines and pestilences" would be among the signs. Poverty and disease are Siamese twins. The problem of food supplies is the major cause of worry in about ninety percent of the nations of the earth. The march of Communism threatens many nations with economic strangulation. Vast population areas are half-starved. Famines result in the loss of millions of lives each year.

Strange pestilences in our generation have baffled the medical world. Notwithstanding the tremendous strides in medical science, there are a great host of maladies which afflict and torment human bodies, resulting in suffering and death. As our age courses toward its end these pestilences shall increase, both in number and intensity.

"Earthquakes in divers places."

The seismologists tell us that earthquakes are more numerous, occurring in all parts of the earth, every day. Every thirty minutes there is a quake somewhere on the surface of the earth, to say nothing of the countless explosions within the earth.

As our earth trembles and quakes, we must be reminded of the inspired Scripture which anticipates the coming of our Lord; "For we know that the whole creation groaneth and travaileth in pain together until now . . . even we ourselves groan within ourselves, waiting for the adoption, to wit, the redemption of our body," (Rom. 8:22,23).

False Christ's and Counterfeit Systems:

Jesus warned, "For many shall come in My name, saying, I am Christ; and shall deceive many". And He said, "Many false prophets shall arise, and shall deceive many," (Matt. 24.5,11). Paul warned: "Now the Spirit speaketh expressly, that in the latter times some shall depart from the faith, giving heed to seducing spirits, and doctrines of demons,'' (1 Tim. 4:1).

Cults, isms, fads, and counterfeit systems which use the *Name* of Christ, but which have departed from His Word, too numerous to mention are rapidly spreading over the world. Men who "depart from the faith" turn readily to false systems—"giving heed to seducing spirits". Such cults as Christian Science, (falsely so-called), Jehovah's Witnesses, Theosophy, Mormonism, Unity, British-Israelism, Humanism, Spiritism,—to mention but a few— all cling to the name "Christian", but deny basic doctrines of our precious faith. Culmination of all false systems will be the personal Antichrist who will be the most clever imitation, as well as antagonist of Christ.

"Iniquity shall abound."

One of the most significant facts of our time is the *aboundingness of sin.* Satan has multiplied his devices to tempt, ensnare, entrap, and engulf the souls of men, women, and children. He knows "that his time is short". There is more carnality, more crime, more lying, more adultery, more drunkenness, more idolatry, and more rebellion against God than at any previous time since God created Adam.

The *mores* and the social standards of a generation ago have broken down and have succumbed to this floodtide of lewdness and indecency. Wholesome family life is vanishing, giving way to easy divorce and selfish living.

An index to the moral turpitude, social disorder, and spiritual declension of our times is revealed in 2 Tim. 3: 1-5:

> "This know also, that in the last days perilous times shall come. For men shall be lovers of their own selves, covetous, boasters, proud, blasphemers, disobedient to parents, unthankful, unholy, without natural affection, truce-breakers, false accusers, inconti-

nent, fierce, despisers of those that are good, traitors, heady, highminded, lovers of pleasures more than lovers of God; having a form of godliness, but denying the power thereof . . .''

"The love of many shall wax cold."

Our Lord declared that a spirit of indifference and lukewarmness would settle down on the church: "Because iniquity shall abound, the love of many shall wax cold." The spirit of the Laodicean church (Revelation 3) is to prevail in most of Christendom. It is described as being "neither hot, nor cold, but lukewarm". Because of this condition—nauseating to God, He said, "I will spew thee out of My mouth".

The proud boast of this church of the end-time is: "I am rich, and increased with goods, and have need of nothing." But the Lord "who looketh on the heart" (and who is knocking at the door for admittance, vs. 20), X-rays the true condition in these lamentable words: "Thou knowest not that thou art wretched, and miserable, and poor, and blind, and naked."

The Profligacy of the Rich.

The abuse of wealth is associated with the prediction of our Lord's return in James 5:1-6. Within the past twenty-five years the number of millionaires has increased by one thousand percent (in our country). Much of this wealth has been obtained through profiteering and speculations. While the Scriptures do not condemn the accumulating of wealth, per se, yet the spirit of covetousness and hoarding is under the frown of Almighty God who requires of all men that they be faithful stewards of their earthly wealth.

The prophecy in James condemns those whose wealth is illgotten, and who live in "wantonness", without regard to the needs of the unfortunate. Today we read of social parties costing as much as $100,000.00; of palatial mansions costing from $3 to $5 million dollars; of pearl necklaces for Persian cats; and of poodle dog banquets! God says this kind of profligacy and wantonness is a sure sign of the "last days", and (vs. 9) that those who are oppressed are to "be patient"—"stablish your hearts: for the coming of the Lord draweth nigh."

"There shall come . . . scoffers."

The doctrine of the Second Coming of Christ, precious to God's faithful people, is but idle talk and sheer fancy to the unbelieving world, and to a very large segment of the professing church. We should not be surprised because such an attitude was specifically prophecied by Peter, 2 Pet. 3:3, 4: "There shall come in the last days scoffers, walking after their own lusts, and saying, Where is the promise of His coming? for since the fathers fell asleep, all things continue as they were from the beginning of creation." Many prominent ministers ridicule the idea of the personal return of our Lord. Many seminaries regard this teaching as foolish fanaticism. Believers, however, should be comforted in the fact that the presence of many scoffers in the world today is a sure harbinger of the soon return of our Lord.

High Speed Locomotion.

"The chariots shall be with flaming torches *in the day of His preparation* . . . the chariots shall rage in the streets, they shall jostle one against another in the broad ways: they shall seem like torches, they shall run like lightnings," Nahum 2:3,4.

"Knowledge shall be increased."

Looking through the prophetic telescope 2500 years ago the prophet Daniel pointed to certain conditions which would characterize the end-time, one of which is: "Knowledge shall be increased," (Dan. 12:4). The fantastic advancement of our twentieth century in every department of learning and the sciences needs no comment. Our fabulous wealth of "new knowledge" in the fields of chemistry, electronics, mechanics, biology, medicine, radio, television, time-saving devices, modern conveniences, and many other departments, serve to remind us that "the time of the end" is near.

Accelerated Travel.

"Many shall run to and fro," (Dan. 12:4). This prophecy suggests a general spirit of restlessness which finds release in much travel. Our modern system of rapid transit—railway, automobile, bus lines, and air transport—has well nigh eliminated such problems as time and space, and has enhanced the desire to travel. "To go places," seems to be the goal of an increasingly large segment of the population. Daniel foresaw this condition, and declared that the time when "many shall run to and fro" would mark the end-time.

Spiritual Blindness of the Wicked.

This same prophet also declared that the end-time would be characterized by the gross spiritual darkness of unbelievers: "But the wicked shall do wickedly, and none of the wicked shall understand," (12:10). In our generation there has never been such an opportunity for the unbelieving world to receive the enlightenment of God's Word, thanks to radio and television which have carried the Gospel to the uttermost parts of the earth. However, it is a lamentable fact that here in America the wicked are more difficult to penetrate and persuade than ever before. And we have learned from many missionaries that the same is increasingly true in other lands. Gross darkness covers the earth, and the end is not yet. "When the Son of man cometh, will He find faith on the earth?"

"The wise shall understand."

In the same prophecy which declared that "none of the wicked shall understand," it is also predicted: "But the wise shall understand." Spiritual discernment is the heritage of those who live in the fellowship of the Holy Spirit. Our Lord rebuked the religious leaders for not being able to "discern the signs of the times". From this statement by our Lord it is known that this quality of fine spiritual discernment on the part of believers is well pleasing to Him, and is moreover the normal atmosphere and experience for God's people. We must remember that when our Lord promised the Holy Spirit, He said, "He shall guide you into all truth . . . He shall take the things that are Mine and show them unto you."

The Apostle Paul emphasized that "eye hath not seen, nor hath ear heard; neither have there entered into the heart of man the things which God has prepared for them that love Him. *But God hath revealed them unto us by His Spirit:* for the Spirit searcheth all things, yea, the deep things of God," (1 Cor. 2:9, 10). The "signs of the times" pertaining to the glorious return of Christ for His people, can be interpreted by those who are truly in fellowship with the Holy Spirit. "The wise shall understand."

The Radiance of True Believers.

"They that be wise shall shine as the brightness of the firmament, and they that turn many to righteousness as the stars forever and ever," (Dan. 12:3). This, we observe is in very close relationship with the above prophecy. Not only shall the wise "understand", but they shall be radiant witnesses. Even as our Lord declared His disciples to be "the light of the world", we are to "shine as lights in the world". What an exalted calling we have here, during the last days of this age when the gross darkness of unbelief covers the earth, and when the great wave of apostasy has all but blacked-out the ministry of the professing church, God's faithful ones can yet shine for Him, and can be instrumental in the winning of many souls.

So, a singular reward is promised: "They that turn many to righteousness (shall shine) as the stars for ever and ever." Remember, also, how our Lord associated the faithful witnessing of His people with His return: "This Gospel of the kingdom shall be preached in all the world for a witness unto all nations; *and then shall the end come.*" (Matt. 24:14).

The "budding fig tree."

It was in answer to the question of His disciples, "when shall these things be? and what shall be the sign of Thy coming, and of the end of the world?" that our Lord gave the parable of the budding fig tree, (Matt. 24:32-34). The fig tree here, as elsewhere, represents the Nation of Israel. The "budding" represents "new life". Clearly, this prophecy concerns the return of Israel to their own land, and their re-nationalization. This stupendous event has now occurred. (See Chapter 6.) Therefore, the tremendous significance of our Lord's explanation of the sign of the end-time: "Now learn a parable of the fig tree: when his branch is yet tender, and putteth forth leaves, ye know that summer is nigh; so likewise ye, when ye shall see all these things, *know that it is near, even at the doors.*" And then He added: *"This generation*—(that is, the generation which should witness the budding of the fig tree)—shall not pass till all these things be fulfilled."

The March of Atheistic Communism and the Anti-God Movement.

The spirit of the antichrist "is even now already in the world," not merely as a philosophy, but as a definite organized militant movement, pressing on with fanatical zeal. (See Chapter 7, and for fuller treatment, the author's book, "Red World Revolution".)

This anti-God spirit will reach its climax when men shall say, "Let us break their bands asunder, and cast away their cords from us," (Psalm 2). At that time God will say, "I have set My King upon My holy hill of Zion". This Satan-inspired rebellion will be broken only by the personal, visible return of Christ.

"As it was in the days of Noah."

It was incredible that none would hear or heed the divine warnings given by Noah that the world was to be destroyed by the great flood. "They did eat, they drank, they married wives, and were given in marriage." These were normal pursuits: there was nothing wrong with these practices, but the tragedy was, they were completely absorbed with these earthly interests, and would not return to God. They continued doing these things "UNTIL THE FLOOD CAME". Then, it was too late!

Oh, the warnings that are being sounded today, not by a single voice, as Noah, but by a host of God's true witnesses, around the world. But men will not repent. "As it was in the days of Noah, so shall it be in the days of the Son of man," (Luke 17:26, 27).

The Readiness of the Faithful Ones.

"And they that were ready went in with Him to the marriage; and the door was shut," (Matt. 25:10). The five wise virgins were ready when the summons came to "go out and meet the bridegroom" because they had oil in their lamps. The door was shut to the foolish virgins because they had "no oil". Oil is the well known symbol of the Holy Spirit; and it is only through the regenerating power of the Holy Spirit that one can be made ready to meet Christ at His coming.

God's faithful children will be sensitive to the call from heaven, "Behold, the Bridegroom cometh: go ye out to meet Him". Remember that Jesus concluded the parable of the ten virgins with the admonition, "Watch, therefore, for ye know neither the day nor the hour wherein the Son of man cometh," (vs. 13). "Surely, I come quickly."

May the closing supplication of the Revelation be the earnest prayer of all God's people as we await the blessed coming of our Lord: "EVEN SO, COME, LORD JESUS!"

XVII Eternal Destiny of the Wicked

Eternal Destiny of the Wicked

We have previously given attention to the two resurrections and the two great future judgments. It is fitting that we should look beyond those judgments to note the two destinies—the destiny of the saved, and the destiny of the lost.

The subject of the eternal destiny of the saved and the lost are generally regarded as doctrinal subjects, as well as prophetic. The revelation of these two eternities as set forth in the sacred Scriptures is accepted and incorporated in the confessions of faith of most Christian bodies, and also by the Jews.

Because certain particulars describing these two destinies are given in the prophetic Scriptures, such as the Book of Revelation, the subject comes well within the limits of prophecy, as well as being didactic or doctrinal teaching. In our study, we make no distinction between the two. It is the revelation of God's Word on the subject with which we are concerned.

We are at first impressed by the vivid contrasts which are drawn. At only one point can it be said that these two destinies are alike, and that is in their eternal character. In every other respect there is a contrast. It is the difference between light and darkness; joy and sorrow; felicity and suffering; tranquility and despair; glorious fellowship and unutterable loneliness; bright and blessed mansions and the flames of torment.

It will be well that we take a look at both these destinies as they are unveiled in the holy Scriptures—Heaven and hell. Jesus had much to say about both. Since the judgment of the Great White Throne is yet fresh in our minds, we shall consider, first, the destiny of the wicked. Concerning these our Lord said, "These shall go away into everlasting punishment". And He said, "There shall be wailing and gnashing of teeth".

No man ever warned so solemnly of hell as Jesus. He said much more about hell than He did about Heaven. He knew what hell is like, and He painted a vivid and lurid picture of the eternal home of the lost and damned. Not only did He warn men, and plead with them to "escape the damnation of hell,"—He did more—-He went to the cross, and suffered as no man ever suffered, Himself bearing the condemnation of the sinner in order to save the sinner from hell.

In describing the horrors of hell, in the 9th chapter of Mark, our Lord warned, in these words:

> "Whosover shall offend one of these little ones that believe in Me, it is better for him that a millstone were hanged about his neck, and he were cast into the sea. And if thy hand offend thee, cut it off: it is better for thee to enter into life maimed, than having two hands to go into hell, into the fire that never shall be quenched; where their worm dieth not, and the fire is not quenched. . . ."

God forbid that I should try to make hell one whit different than it is described by our blessed Lord! If Jesus felt the urgency to speak so freely, and with solemn warning about the destiny of the wicked, why should we ever try to picture hell as less horrible? What an awful judgment will be upon those preachers who leave hell out of their pulpit vocabulary!

At this point, I desire to read you from the 16th chapter of Luke's Gospel the most fearful description of hell that has ever been given. Our Lord told the story of two men who lived on this earth, and died. This is not a parable—

although it would not be less real if it were—but it is a narrative of something which actually happened, and the true names of the men are given. He said:

"There was a certain rich man, which was clothed in purple and fine linen, and fared sumptuously every day: and there was a certain beggar named Lazarus, which was laid at his gate, full of sores, and desiring to be fed with the crumbs which fell from the rich man's table: moreover, the dogs came and licked his sores. And it came to pass, that the beggar died, and was carried by the angels into Abraham's bosom: the rich man died and was buried: and in hades he lift up his eyes, being in torments, and seeth Abraham afar off, and Lazarus, in his bosom. And he cried and said, Father Abraham, have mercy on me, and send Lazarus, that he may dip the tip of his finger in water, and cool my tongue; for I am tormented in this flame. But Abraham said, Son, remember that thou in thy lifetime receivedst thy good things, and likewise Lazarus evil things: but now he is comforted, and thou art tormented. Beside all this, between us and you there is a great gulf fixed; so that they which would pass from hence to you cannot; neither can they pass to us, that would come from thence. Then he said, I pray thee therefore, father; that thou wouldest send him to my father's house; for I have five brethren; that he may testify unto them, lest they also come into this place of torment. Abraham saith unto him, They have Moses and the prophets; let them hear them. And he said, Nay, father Abraham; but if one went unto them from the dead, they will repent. And he said unto him, If they hear not Moses and the prophets, neither will they be persuaded, though one rose from the dead."

Certain awful facts stand out in this description of the home of the damned. The people there are alive and conscious—possessing all their faculties. They can reason, and remember, and know why they are there, and can suffer remorse, and can endure physical and mental torment, and can see, and look up into Heaven, and recognize people in glory, and can know of their bliss. They can plead for help, but know that their case is utterly hopeless. They thirst for water, with no relief. They suffer the torment of the flames in eternal despair.

"In hell he lifted up his eyes, being in torments." Oh, lost man, lost woman, think of plunging into that sea of flames, with the horrible realization that you are in hell forever! Oh, think of entering the abode of doomed spirits who will never see daylight again. Think of being conscious that "a great gulf is fixed", so that there can never be so much as a ray of hope that you can ever escape.

Think of realizing, one minute after you have entered hell, that this is the place that was prepared for the devil and his angels. Think of realizing that Jesus Christ went to the cross to save you from that terrible doom!

Your associates will be a world of demons. Besides, there will be the hosts of Christ-rejecting souls who on this earth lived in sin, and died in their unregenerate state. You will be among the vilest people who ever lived —the sorcerers, the idolators, the murderers, the adulterers, the whoremongers, the blasphemers, the liars, the crooks and the robbers, the coarse, the vulgar, the mean and the hateful, the vicious and the cruel—and every conceivable kind of depraved humanity. They will be your associates. There will be no born-again Christians there, not one. There will be no one there to help you, or to love you; no one you can call your friend. "In hades he lifted up his eyes, being in torments."

"Have mercy on me," was the plea of this man in hell, as he looked up into the face of Abraham. But he waited too long to pray. He had gone to a place where prayers are without effect. If he had offered that same prayer while he was yet on this earth, he would have been instantly heard. That was the prayer of the publican, "Have mercy on me"—a prayer which the Lord heard, and the publican was saved—justified—because he offered that prayer, and put his faith in the Saviour.

Millions of others have been saved who have offered that prayer. I can testify that today I am speaking to you because I once offered that prayer, and the Lord heard me. I declare to you who hear me today that you can be saved this minute, instantly, if you will offer that prayer in sincerity: "Lord, have mercy on me." No, my friend, you do not have to go to that awful place of eternal torment. God is "not willing that any should perish, but that all should come to repentance." But do not forget the word of Jesus, in Luke 13:3: "Except ye repent, ye shall all likewise perish."

Abraham replied to this man in hell. He said, "Son, remember". He reminded him of his failure to repent while he was on the earth. He had every opportunity which Lazarus had, and more, but he chose rather to live selfishly and in unbelief; and so he died, as he had lived—in unbelief.

"Son, remember." Oh, think of the memories that this man must have had—memories of all the opportunities he had by-passed; memories of all those impulses he must have felt when he was urged to believe in the God of Lazarus, the beggar, and serve Him; memories of all his sins—his pride, his lying, his pleasure-loving, Christ-rejecting life; memories of his misspent hours, and days, and months, and years—a misspent life. Memories, memories, memories—bitter, harrassing, remorseful, horrible memories. "Son, remember."

Think of spending an eternity in hell with nothing to do but remember. Some of you will remember the patient efforts of a kind and loving father, or mother, in seeking to bring you to Jesus. Some will remember the minister who made the message plain, and you were urged to go forward and confess Christ, but you would not. Some will remember the Sunday school teacher, or the friend who urged you to accept Christ. Many of you will remember the earnest message of your radio minister, urging you to yield to Christ. There will no doubt be some members of this very radio audience in hell who will remember this message, urging you to accept the Lord Jesus Christ.

God forbid that hell should include you, my friend. Trust Him now, and be saved forever. "Whosoever shall call upon the name of the Lord shall be saved." "Him that cometh unto Me, I will in no wise cast out."

XVIII Eternal Destiny of the Righteous

Eternal Destiny of the Righteous

Our Lord promised, "I go to prepare a place for you, and if I go and prepare a place for you, I will come again, and receive you unto Myself; that where I am there ye may be also . . . And whither I go ye know, and the way ye know," (John 14: 2-4.)

Jesus taught that all believers will go to Heaven. "I am the resurrection and the life: he that believeth in Me, though he were dead, yet shall he live." "For God so loved the world that He gave His only begotten Son, that whosoever believeth in Him should not perish, but have everlasting life."

He urged upon His disciples to be faithful so that they may receive that welcome plaudit: "Well done, thou good and faithful servant; thou hast been faithful over a few things: I will make thee ruler over many. Enter thou into the joy of thy Lord." He urged "Lay up for yourselves treasures in Heaven, where neither moth nor rust doth corrupt, and where thieves do not break through and steal."

Heaven is in view in all the parables of the kingdom which our Lord gave. Heaven is the goal toward which the children of God move, as the place of their eternal destiny.

It was given to John the Beloved, on the Isle of Patmos, to behold the beauties of Heaven, and to transmit to us the radiant glory and supernal blessedness of the Home of God's redeemed family. May we draw aside the curtain, and take a glimpse or two of that heavenly land.

Think of the unspeakable splendor of our eternal Home! There are the walls of jasper, representing the glory of God. There are the twelve foundation stones of various colors, which much suggest the manifold manifestations of God's glory. The city itself is of gold, which speaks of the righteousness of God. The gates of pearl are symbolic of the church which is "the pearl of great price", spoken of by our Lord in the parable. The streets are of transparent gold, and this suggests that there is no defilement there, all is purity.

And how spacious is that eternal city! Twelve thousand furlongs each way, or a cube that is almost 1500 miles each way. Plenty of room there. "In my Father's house are many mansions." There will be ample room for all who dwell there. Some one has calculated mathematically that had every one been saved from Adam's time until now, there would be room enough, and to spare, in the city of the New Jerusalem.

Heaven will be illuminated by the glory of God and of the Lamb. There will be no need of created light. No light of sun or moon, but the light of the Shekinah glory: That same glory that outshone the noonday sun by which Saul of Tarsus was overwhelmed on the Damascus road. That same light that overshadowed the mercy seat behind the veil. That same light that Peter and James and John beheld on the Mount of Transfiguration. The light of the glory of God. "And the city had no need of sun, neither of the moon, to shine in it: for the glory of God did lighten it, and the Lamb is the light thereof."

In Heaven there will be divine companionship. "And I heard a great voice out of Heaven, saying, Behold the tabernacle of God is with men, and He will dwell with them, and they shall be His people, and God Himself shall be with them, and be their God." In the garden of Eden, God dwelt with and companioned with Adam and Eve, before sin brought about the separation. In a very real sense, God was with the children of Israel in the wilderness, though they did not behold Him. In a very real sense God walked among men in the person of His Son while on earth, though His glory was veiled by His flesh, for He was "the brightness of His glory, and the express image of His person", and "in Him was all the fulness of the Godhead bodily". And throughout this dispensation God dwells with us by His Spirit. But in a still more wonderful sense shall God dwell with us in that eternal home. There will be the most intimate companionship with Him there!

There shall also be the blessed reunion with loved ones who have gone on before us, and in Heaven love shall be made perfect. With this, also, there shall be the unending fellowship with all the saints of God!

These things will be made blessed because the curse of sin will not be known there. "And God shall wipe away all tears from their eyes; and there shall be no more death, neither sorrow nor crying, neither shall there be any more pain, for the former things are passed away!" No more heartaches, no more disappointments, no more grief, no more pain, no more death, no more coffins, no more hearses, no more cemeteries, no more gravestones, no more crepe on the door, no more tears, no more of saying goodbye to loved ones and friends! The former things are passed away!

There will be the throne of God in the midst, and the eternal reign of love. And our only occupation will be to serve Him. It shall be one endless day of glory. "There shall be no night there." And it shall be "forever and ever".

Such is the Home that Jesus is preparing for us, and such is the Home to which He will carry His own when He comes for us. It is blessed to contemplate it; it is glorious to meditate upon it. Down here in this world of trials and of heartaches, there can be nothing more heartening than a constant vision of our eternal home. As pilgrims and sojourners we are journeying toward our rightful inheritance; as Abraham of old, we "look for a city which hath foundations, whose builder and maker is God". This world is not our home, for "our citizenship is in Heaven", and our Father is there!

There was a boy travelling through the West, and it was a long journey over the burning desert sands. He sat alone in the railway train; and it was a very hot day. The sun burned down almost in blazing heat, and the dust filled the car. Other passengers seemed to notice that the boy in his loneliness was happy and more contented than the rest. As he looked out over the trackless sands he seemed to see what no one else saw. At length a lady came to him and leaning over she said, "My boy, I have been thinking about you today. Do you not get very tired taking this long, hot journey?" "Well," he said, "I do not think I am very tired. It is hot and dusty, and it is more than I thought it would be, but I am happy. I am happy because my father is going to meet me at the end of the journey". Our way cannot become dreary when we carry with us the vision of Heaven, and the assurance that our Heavenly Father will welcome us over there.

Jesus said, "I go to prepare a place for you, and if I go to prepare a place for you, I will come again and receive you unto Myself, that where I am there ye may be also."

> When I can read my title clear
> To mansions in the skies,
> I'll bid farewell to every fear,
> And wipe my weeping eyes.
>
> Should earth against my soul engage,
> And fiery darts be hurled,

Then I can smile at Satan's rage,
And face a frowning world.

Let cares like a wild deluge come,
And storms of sorrow fall,
May I but safely reach my home,
My God, my heaven, my all.

There shall I bathe my weary soul
In seas of heavenly rest,
And not a wave of trouble roll
Across my peaceful breast.

Do you have an inheritance up there? Do you have a mansion in the Father's house?

Some day, we who are God's children, are going to take a trip. We are going to leave this world, and go to Heaven. We may think of it as a long trip, and yet, in reality, it is only a short trip, for it will take us such a short time to get there. One minute we will be on this earth, the next minute in glory. In fact, less time than this, for the Scripture measures the time element—as, "the twinkling of an eye".

The scientific world is now building artificial planets, and dreaming of space ships which will provide transportation to the moon. However, all the efforts of men, regardless of how successful they may appear to be, will amount to little more than the effort of the builders of ancient Babel—for their purpose was to build a tower that would reach unto Heaven.

We shall not need a space ship made by the hands of men to carry us into the presence of God, and into our eternal Home. When God calls you, or me, to "Come up hither", there will be no transportation problem, and no fare to pay. Jesus said, "I will come again, and receive you unto Myself."

And, it is a wonderful fact that Heaven cannot be thought of as being a strange place, because Jesus has designated it as our eternal Home, and He said, "that where I am, there ye may be also". It can never be a strange place, for He will be there to provide us with His constant companionship.

Most of us have loved ones there, and it will be like going home to be with them again. Our earthly homes are often disrupted by the forces of sin. The world and the flesh and the devil—that unholy trinity—often combine to interrupt and to destroy our home life on this earth. But in Heaven love will be made perfect. And nothing will enter in to mar our happiness.

The abundant resources of Heaven shall be placed at our disposal, and we shall have everything that we will need and desire. There will be no economic problems. There will be no domestic or social problems. There will be no moral problems. Everything will be perfect.

And we know that Heaven will be a wonderful place, also, because there will be such wonderful people there. All the choice souls of this world, of all generations— all who have been washed in the blood of the Lamb, and have been clothed with the spotless righteousness of God; all the people who have been filled with the Spirit of God, and who have exemplified His lovely qualities; all the people in whose hearts the love of God dwells— all will be there. Thank God for the glorious prospect of being ushered into the presence and fellowship of millions upon millions of such people—the saints of God.

And, there will be the angels. Oh, how we have wanted to know more about the angels! They are certainly among God's loveliest creatures. The angels will be our companions in glory, and perhaps our teachers concerning the wonders of God's great universe.

All these will be there to greet us on our arrival at the gates of pearl, and they will give to us the most resplendent welcome that can be provided by our loving Heavenly Father. And Jesus, our adorable Lord and Saviour, will be on the Throne of His glory, and what a thrill to see His face, and to join the hosts of Heaven in singing His incessant praises.

As the inspired Apostle said, ''Eye hath not seen; nor hath ear heard; neither hath there entered into the heart of man the things which God hath prepared for them that love Him.''

And to think that all these glories will be entered into in the space of only a moment of time!

> Think of stepping on shore,
>   And finding it Heaven;
> Of taking hold of a hand,
>   And finding it God's hand;
> Of breathing a new air,
>   And finding it celestial air;
> Of feeling invigorated,
>   And finding it immortality;
> Of passing from storm and tempest
>   To a perfect calm;
> Of waking, and knowing
>   That I am Home!

How close some of us may be to that wonderful moment, we cannot know.

XIX "One Shall Be Taken, the Other Left"

"One Shall Be Taken, the Other Left"

It is not surprising that we should raise the question, "What will the coming of the Lord Jesus Christ be like?" This question was directed to Jesus by His disciples, in more explicit terms. Their question: "Tell us, when shall these things be? and what shall be the sign of Thy coming, and of the end of the world?" (Matt. 24:3)

Our Lord responded to their curiosity, because He felt that they should know the answer to these questions. The first 31 verses of the 24th chapter of Matthew describe the character of this age, and the signs which should precede Christ's return, clear up to the time of His personal revelation. Then, as if to amplify and clarify, Jesus gave the parable of the fig tree, and added the word, "This generation shall not pass till all these things be fulfilled." And He said, "But of that day and hour knoweth no man, no, not the angels of heaven, but My Father only."

Now to emphasize the indifference and unbelief of the generation which should witness His coming, Jesus drew a comparison. He said: "As the days of Noah were, so shall also the coming of the Son of man be. For as in the days that were before the flood, they were eating and drinking, marrying and giving in marriage, until the day that Noah entered the ark, and *knew not* until the flood came, and took them all away."

The point of emphasis here, is that those people of Noah's generation were engaged in normal pursuits, without regard to God's warning of judgment. They were not condemned for "eating and drinking" nor for "marrying and giving in marriage." These were perfectly normal pursuits. But the tragedy was, they were indifferent to God's warning to repent.

They refused to believe that judgment would come. They were indifferent. They were unconcerned. Now, Jesus said, this kind of attitude would be repeated during the generation when He comes. He said, "So also shall the coming of the Son of man be."

Then, our Lord proceeded to give a vivid description of what would take place. Just as *"suddenness"* character-ized the visitation of judgment in Noah's day, so will sud-denness mark the last hour of this present age. The day of His coming, in all outward appearances, will be like any other day. But, suddenly, two shall be working to-gether in the field, and "the one shall be taken, and the other left." Two women shall be grinding at the mill: "the one shall be taken, the other left."

It shall all happen so quickly, even as "the twinkling of an eye." That is only a split second of time. Should any one of my hearers ask the question, "Why will His coming be so sudden? why without warning?" The answer is, is it *not* without warning. Now, for nineteen centuries the Gospel has been preached, and every true messenger of Christ has sounded the warning of the coming judgment. (You will see that I qualify my statement—every *true* messenger of Christ sounds the warning. For there are many today who never speak of repentence, or of the hor-rible judgments to come upon an unbelieving, Christ-re-jecting world. No sermons on the flaming justice of God to be unleashed on a rebellious race. No sermons on retri-bution. No sermons on hell.)

God does have His faithful witnesses who are pro-claiming the whole counsel of God. And by means of radio and television more multiplied millions of souls are being invited into the overtures of God's everlasting mercy through the Gospel of the Lord Jesus Christ, and, at the same time, being warned of the inevitable judgments to come. But men are more indifferent, more callous-hearted, more rebellious than ever. Upon all such the judgment will suddenly fall. Yes, the coming of Christ will be sudden.

And, His coming is also characterized by a great *separation*. "The one shall be taken, the other left." Please listen to me, you who have an unsaved husband, or unsaved wife. You love that companion, and you hope to be with that dear one in eternity. Let me tell you, when God's hour hand strikes for the moment of Christ's return, there will be a separation, and it shall be a complete separation, and it shall occur so quickly that you will not have time to say Goodbye.

Do you have a sister or a brother who is not ready to go up in the rapture? How awful to think of an eternal separation! "The one shall be taken, and the other left." Do you have precious children who are not saved? Oh, what a fearful thought, to consider that if Christ should come today, the separation from them would be so sudden, and for all eternity! Those friends who are lost, and those cherished neighbors—think of being separated from them suddenly and forever! "The one shall be taken, and the other left."

I have imagined the scene of a wife, waiting for her husband to come in from work, but he never gets home, because caught up in the rapture. Or, the scene of a husband, rising in the morning to the alarm clock, and finding his wife gone—caught up in the rapture.

Or, the scene of children coming in from school, never to see their parents again. Or, the scene at a railway station where there is to be a meeting of a precious mother, or father; but the meeting never takes place, because the parents were ready for the rapture. Or, have you thought of what it will be like, when the office opens, or the department store, or the shop, or the industrial plant—with a sizeable percentage of the employees missing, and all the rest who remain discussing the strange events.

Many a surgical operation will not be performed, because Christian doctors are snatched away. Many an airliner will not reach its destination, because the pilot at the controls was ready for the summons. Think what it will be like on ten thousand highways, with horrible tragedies everywhere, because born-again Christians were snatched away in the twinkling of an eye. Radio and television stations will blaze the news of multiplied tragedies and calls for "missing persons" twenty-four hours a day. But some stations will go off the air. Newspapers will do a land-office business with extras, sending forth the greatest news stories ever printed. Telegraphic offices will be stampeded. Telephone operators will be bombarded. Many calls will not be executed.

Many professing Christians will be left behind, because all they could show was a meaningless church membership. They will gather by the thousands at the churches, but doubtless most of the ministers will have gone up in the rapture. However, there will be many ministers who will be left behind, and they will try to console the sorrowing ones, by delivering smooth orations of false philosophy. These are the ones of whom Jesus warned, "In that day many shall say unto Me, 'Lord, Lord, have we not prophecied in Thy name' . . . and I will say unto them, 'I never knew you.'" "The one shall be taken, and the other left."

Oh, there will be so many *surprises* for the folks left behind—left to face the inevitable judgments of God. Doubtless, most sinners will recognize immediately that they were left behind because they had rejected Jesus Christ. But in their company there will be those whom they would have believed were prepared to meet God. They will look upon Mr. Moralist, and say, "I am surprised that he did not go away in the rapture. He lived such a good, exemplary life; never drank liquor, never gambled, never swore." In their company will be a great philanthropist, who has given big sums of money to charity, and they will say, "Surely this person should have made the grade." They will look upon Mrs. Social Butterfly, and say, "This person had such a winsome personality. She had so many, many friends, and was kind and good to all. Why didn't she get in the rapture?" Then, they will turn to Mr. Political Leader, and say, "Why are you here? Your whole life was devoted to the uplift of society."

And, of course, many will be surprised to find some preachers and church workers left behind. They did not make the rapture—all for the same reason! They were not born-again Christians. Some will doubtless get out their New Testaments and read from the 3rd chapter of John the words of Jesus, "Except a man be born again, he cannot see the kingdom of God." Oh, my friends, how can we be so unconcerned in the face of such plain warnings from the Word of God, and from the Son of God Himself? Jesus warned of the suddenness of His coming, and of the dreadful separations, and of the surprises. He drives home to His hearers the urgency of this event with two illustrations. He speaks here of the surprise of the thief entering the house, and despoiling it. And He said this could only happen because the master of the house was not on the alert. Here are His words: "But know this, if the goodman of the house had known in what watch the thief would come, he would have watched, and would not have suffered his house to be broken up."

Then follows the warning, "Therefore be ye also ready: for in such an hour as ye think not the Son of man cometh." Next, Jesus gave the parable of the "faithful and wise servant." Note carefully the warning expressed to the servant who foolishly said, "My Lord delayeth his coming'': ''Who then is a faithful and wise servant, whom his lord hath made ruler over his household, to give them meat in due season? Blessed is that servant, whom his lord when he cometh shall find so doing. Verily I say unto you, That he shall make him ruler over all his goods. But and if that evil servant shall say in his heart, My lord delayeth his coming; and shall begin to smite his fellowservants, and to eat and drink with the drunken; the lord of that servant shall come in a day when he looketh not for him, and in an hour that he is not aware of, And shall cut him asunder, and appoint him his portion with the hypocrites: there shall be weeping and gnashing of teeth'' (Matt. 24:45-51).

Trust Him now and be saved before it is too late—remembering that God ''is not willing that any should perish, but that all should come to repentance,'' . . . ''for God so loved the world that He gave His only begotten Son, that whosoever believeth in Him should not perish, but have everlasting life.''

XX "Prepare to Meet Thy God"

"Prepare to Meet Thy God"

This chapter is added for one class of people: the unsaved. Although the simplicity of God's way of salvation is explained in other chapters, the author feels compelled to make this direct approach to any, and to all who are not ready to meet Christ at His coming.

In view of the overwhelming evidence of the soon consummation of all things, hence the closing of the day of mercy for sinful men, it behooves all to be ready at the return of our Lord. Those who are *not* ready, we urge to *get ready*. In the language of the prophet Amos, "Prepare to meet thy God," (Amos 4:12).

May I speak to you most personally! You *can* escape the dreadful judgments described in this book. You *can* be ready to meet the Son of God at His coming. You *can* meet Him unashamed and without fear. You can have the full assurance of faith. You can have the peace of God in your heart. You can have joy in the anticipation of His coming! And I want to tell you how all this is possible.

There is only one reason why anyone is unready for Christ's coming. One, and only one thing causes a chasm between one's soul and the God who made us. This we know is SIN. The Bible reveals God as a holy God and proclaims His intense hatred for sin. His Word shows us plainly that God can never enter into fellowship with the sinner until the sin question has been settled. The Bible reveals that He is a just God, and because of His sheer justness, He must punish sin. Every sinner must stand before His presence. And this includes the entire human race, for it is written, "ALL have sinned and come short of the glory of God," (Rom. 3:23).

173

Every intelligent creature knows that he is accountable to God. "So then every one of us must give account of himself to God " (Rom. 14:12). When we consider the awful penalty of sin as prescribed by a just God, we cannot but sense the terribleness of that day of accountability to those who are lost. God has such intense hatred for sin, He has declared that "the soul that sinneth, it shall die " (Ezek. 18:4); and, "The wages of sin is death " (Rom. 6:23). He has shown us that this death for the sinner means eternal separation from God, and that the sinner shall forever suffer in a hell which was prepared for the devil and his angels.

The Bible reveals that God has already pronounced this condemnation ("condemned already" John 3:18), and that every sinner is already under the wrath of God—"the wrath of God abideth on him" John 3:36. This puts the sinner's case in a hopeless condition, so far as is his ability to do anything about it. There is utterly no way that the sinner can appease God, or win His favor. There is utterly no way of escape for the sinner. One who has a sinful nature can never please God. Because the penalty of sin is death, and the judgment has already been pronounced, there is no hope for the sinner to save himself.

But I have good news for you: (the word "Gospel" mean "good news") and it may be stated in four words: GOD LOVES THE SINNER. And because of His love He has, in infinite mercy, provided the means of redemption for the sinner, and offers salvation and eternal life to every sinner!

This glorious fact is true only because God's Son was willing to take the sinner's place in death. It was for this cause, and this cause alone, that the Son of God left heaven's glory, came to this earth, identified Himself with our race, through the virgin birth. For, it is written that, "When the fulness of time was come, God sent forth His

Son, made of a woman, made under the law, to redeem them that were under the (condemnation of) the law, that we might receive the adoption of sons,'' (Gal. 4:4,5). Also: "Christ hath redeemed us from the curse of the law, being made a curse for us: for it is written, Cursed is every one that hangeth on a tree," (Gal. 3:13). Jesus said, "FOR THIS CAUSE I CAME INTO THE WORLD".

This mighty truth is so clearly revealed in John 3:14,15: "For as Moses lifted up the serpent in the wilderness, even so must the Son of man be lifted up, that whosoever believeth in Him should not perish, but have everlasting life." Seven hundred years before Christ went to the cross the Prophet Isaiah wrote of His death for sinners: "He was wounded for our transgressions, He was bruised for our iniquities: the chastisement of our peace was upon Him: and with His stripes we are healed . . . the Lord hath laid on Him the iniquity of us all," (Isa. 53:5,6).

The deep, eternal meaning of the atonement is that Christ in His death on the cross expiated the penalty of our guilt. This means that He fully and forever satisfied the law of God on our behalf, so that when the sinner—any sinner—believes on Christ as his divine Substitute, and trusts Him as Lord and Saviour, he is immediately delivered from the curse and condemnation of sin, and is no longer under the wrath of God, but is acquitted forever, forgiven, set free, and accepted into the family of God. In His dying moments Christ declared, "It is finished". It is therefore a finished transaction!

This provision for salvation has been made for every sinner on earth: "For God so loved the WORLD that He gave His only begotten Son, that WHOSOEVER believeth in Him should not perish, but have everlasting life," (John 3:16). "WHOSOEVER shall call up on the name of the Lord shall be saved," (Rom. 10:13).

In view of the tremendous price paid for our redemption, is it not strange that men through unbelief seek to alter God's plan by "adding to" or by "taking from" the clear and simple revelation of the Gospel? What an unspeakable offense to God to despise the cross, or seek to save one's self through "good works", man-made standards, ethics, and religions. "For if righteousness come by the law," (or, by the effort to keep the law), "then Christ is dead in vain," (Gal. 2:21).

My unsaved friend, you have a Saviour, the living and eternal Saviour. He is your Friend. He died for you, on your behalf, in your place, that you might be forever saved. "Greater love hath no man than this, that a man lay down His life for His friends," (John 15:13). Triumphing over death, as He did on the third day, He is your living Saviour. "Wherefore, He is able also to save them to the uttermost that come unto God by Him, seeing He ever liveth to make intercession for them," (Heb. 7:25). "Neither is there salvation in any other: for there is none other name under heaven given among men whereby we must be saved," (Acts 4:12).

And, now, He extends to you a personal invitation: "Come unto Me, and I will give you rest," (Matt. 11:28). "Behold, I stand at the door, and knock: if any man will hear My voice, and open the door, I will come in to him, and will sup with him, and he with Me," (Rev. 3:20). Trust Him now, and be saved forever, for "there is no condemnation to them which are in Christ Jesus," (Rom. 8:1). With Christ as your Saviour and Lord, you need never fear the judgments which are to fall on the unbelieving world, but you will be ready for Christ at His coming; and you, too, will learn to pray, "Even so, come, Lord Jesus".

"THEREFORE, PREPARE TO MEET THY GOD!"